"A landmark work of social psychology."
Booklist

"One simply can't finish this book and see the world in the same way."
ALAN DERSHOWITZ
Harvard Law School

"Dr. Langer's seminal work on mindful behavior has broad implications for aviation safety and the development of proper roles for humans vs. machines."
CLAY FOUSHEE
Chief Scientific and Technical Advisor
Federal Aviation Authority

"One of the most provocative books that this reviewer has seen in a long time....Engaging, relevant, and concise, moving smartly from point to point."
Brain/Mind Bulletin

"A truly pioneering study of the dangers and damage of mindlessness and loss of control over one's life; for women and men in age, in corporations and/or in the professions."
BETTY FRIEDAN

"Langer not only challenges us to reach for our untapped reserves, she also shows ways to make this possible."
PAUL BALTES
Max Planck Institute for Human Development and Education, Berlin

"Whether you're an educator, homemaker, business person, mental health worker...differently abled or abled, young or old, there is something in this book for you."
Deaf Community News

"In my seminar on advanced social psychology, *Mindfulness* stimulated wonderfully lively discussion."
ROGER BROWN
Harvard University

"Langer demonstrates a rare capacity both to see what is extraordinary about human events and to envision even more enlivening human possibilities."
LEE ROSS
Stanford University

"One is reminded, reading these pages, of Freud's *Psychopathology of Everyday Life* and of Hannah Arendt's *The Banality of Evil*. Like those pioneering books, this one 'naturalizes' a human scourge—everyday functional stupidity in this case—and makes it not only comprehensible but also subject to change."
JEROME BRUNER,
author of *Actual Minds, Possible Worlds*

Ellen J. Langer

Mindfulness

A MERLOYD LAWRENCE BOOK
LIFELONG BOOKS • DA CAPO PRESS
A Member of the Perseus Books Group

Library of Congress Cataloging-in-Publication Data

Langer, Ellen J., 1947-
    Mindfulness.
    "A Merloyd Lawrence book"
    Includes Index.
    1. Attention. 2. Consciousness. I. Title.
BF321.L23   1989   153   88-33293
ISBN-13 978-0-201-52341-6
ISBN-10 0-201-52341-8

Da Capo Press is a member of the Perseus Books Group.

Cover design by Suzanne Heiser
Text design by Jennie Bush, Designworks, Inc.

Da Capo Press books are available at special discounts for bulk purchases in the United States by corporations, institutions, and other organizations. For more information, please contact the Special Markets Department at the Perseus Books Group, 11 Cambridge Center, Cambridge, MA 02142, call (617)252-5298 or email special.markets@perseusbooks.com.

Find us on the World Wide Web at
www.dacapopress.com

DHSB 50 49 48 47 46 45 44 43 42 41 40 39 38

To the memory of my mother and grandmother

*

Contents

*

Acknowledgments

Because I have written and rewritten this book many times, each time trying to make the ideas of interest to a broader audience, and each time enlisting the patient advice of friends and colleagues, I have many people to thank. Robert Abelson, Daryl Bem, Anne Bernays, Otto Brodtrick, Jerome Bruner, Marjorie Garber, Roslyn Garfield, William Goode, John Hallowell, Gerald Holton, Philip Holzman, Barbara Johnson, Jerome Kagan, Aron Katz, Phyllis Katz, Barbara Levine, Beverly London, Letty Cottin Pogrebin, Helen Rees, Eric Rofes, Howard Stevenson, Phyllis Temple, Marjorie Weiner, and Lenore Weitzman have all enriched the book with their perceptive comments. It is an understatement to say that I am grateful for their help. To Elaine Noble I am especially grateful for rich insights on the relationship between mindlessness/mindfulness theory and alcoholism. The technical aspects of preparing this manuscript were carried out with great proficiency by Julie Viens, Barbara Burg, and Andrea Marcus.

Major concepts used in this book are derived from

research conducted over the past fifteen years, at Yale, City University of New York, and, for the past twelve years, in the Department of Psychology at Harvard. I am therefore deeply indebted to all the people who collaborated with me on these investigations. Most especially I have profited from years of continued collaboration with Benzion Chanowitz.

My ideas sometimes get the better of me. Before I clearly explain one, another comes to mind and seizes my attention. For this reason, I imagine the reader shares my deep gratitude for Merloyd Lawrence's editorial skills, which have been invaluable in shaping this book.

*

Mindfulness

CHAPTER 1

*

Introduction

I don't like the idea of a unitary subject; I prefer the
play of a kaleidoscope: you give it a tap and the little
bits of colored glass form a new pattern.
ROLAND BARTHES, *The Grain of the Voice*

*

One day, at a nursing home in Connecticut, elderly
residents were each given a choice of houseplants to
care for and were asked to make a number of small
decisions about their daily routines. A year and a half
later, not only were these people more cheerful, active,
and alert than a similar group in the same institution
who were not given these choices and responsibilities,
but many more of them were still alive. In fact, less
than half as many of the decision-making, plant-mind-
ing residents had died as had those in the other group.
This experiment, with its startling results, began over
ten years of research into the powerful effects of what
my colleagues and I came to call *mindfulness*, and of its
counterpart, the equally powerful but destructive state
of *mindlessness*.[1]

Unlike the exotic "altered states of consciousness" that we read so much about, mindfulness and mindlessness are so common that few of us appreciate their importance or make use of their power to change our lives. This book is about the psychological and physical costs we pay because of pervasive mindlessness and, more important, about the benefits of greater control, richer options, and transcended limits that mindfulness can make possible.

Although the results of this research have been published in a series of scholarly articles, I have long wanted to present their implications to a wider audience. The benefits of becoming more mindful seem to me too valuable to remain hidden in the archives of social psychology. Every time I receive a request for a reprint of a journal article from a business executive or newspaper reporter, I wish that I could run it through an instant translation machine that would expunge the jargon and statistics and reveal the underlying practical implications of the results. This book, while far from "instant" in the making, is a translation of over fifty experiments and an attempt to demonstrate their implications beyond the lab, both in literature and in daily life.

My first experience of the grave risks of mindlessness occurred while I was in graduate school. My grandmother complained to her doctors about a snake crawling around beneath her skull and giving her headaches. Her descriptions were vivid and figurative, not literal. That was just the way she talked. But the young doctors who took care of her paid little attention to what this very old lady from another culture was telling them. They diagnosed senility. Senility comes with old age, after all, and makes people talk nonsense. When she grew more confused and unhappy, they recommended electroconvulsive therapy ("shock treatment") and convinced my mother to give her approval.

Not until an autopsy was performed did anyone detect my grandmother's brain tumor. I shared my mother's agony and guilt. But who were we to question the doctors? For years afterward I kept thinking about the doctors' reactions to my grandmother's complaints, and about our reactions to the doctors. They went through the motions of diagnosis, but were not open to what they were hearing. Mindsets about senility interfered. We did not question the doctors; mindsets about experts interfered. Eventually, as I continued my work in social psychology, I saw some of the reasons for our errors and this led me further into the study of mindless behavior.

Social psychologists usually look for the ways in which behavior depends on context. When mindless, however, people treat information as though it were *context-free*—true regardless of circumstances. For example, take the statement: Heroin is dangerous. How true is this for a dying individual in intolerable pain?

Once alerted to the dangers of mindlessness and to the possibility of bringing about a more mindful attitude by such deceptively simple measures as those used in the nursing home experiment, I began to see this double-edged phenomenon at work in many different settings. For instance, consider the events that led to the 1982 crash of an Air Florida plane that killed seventy-four passengers. It was a routine flight from Washington, D.C., to Florida with an experienced flight crew. Pilot and copilot were in excellent physical health. Neither was tired, stressed, or under the influence. What went wrong? An extensive examination pointed to the crew's pre-takeoff control checks. As the copilot calls out each control on his list, the pilot makes sure the switches are where he wants them to be. One of these controls is an anti-icer. On this day, the pilot and copilot went over each of the controls as they had always done. They went through their routine and checked "off" when the anti-icer was mentioned. This time, however, the flight was different from their experience. This time they were not flying in the usual warm southern weather. It was icy outside.

As he went through the control checks, one by one as he always did, the pilot appeared to be thinking when he was not.[2] The pre-takeoff routines of pilot and copilot have a lot in common with the tiresome safety demonstrations of flight attendants to experienced, glassy-eyed passengers. When we blindly follow routines or unwittingly carry out senseless orders, we are acting like automatons, with potentially grave consequences for ourselves and others.

We do not all allow ourselves to become mindless. Some concert pianists memorize their music away from the keyboard so as to avoid the predicament in which their fingers "know" the music but they do not. In essence, these experts are keeping themselves mindful for their recitals. In the absence of the keyboard they cannot take their performance for granted.

In the chapters that follow I will demonstrate how and why mindlessness develops, and show how we can become more mindful and oriented in the present in widely differing aspects of our lives. Chapter 2 examines the nature of mindlessness and its relation to similar concepts such as habit and the unconscious. Chapter 3 explores the causes of mindlessness, including the vital role of context, and the nature of our early education. An overview of the costs of mindlessness, the limitations it sets on our skills, and expectations and potential follows in Chapter 4. In Chapter 5, I discuss the nature of mindfulness and distinguish it from related concepts found in Eastern philosophy. Chapters 6 through 10 show the applications of mindfulness research in five major areas of ordinary life: aging, creativity, work, the problem of prejudice, and health.

Those parts of my research that I've particularly enjoyed thinking about, including managing uncertainty in the workplace and the link between mindlessness and the old trap of mind/body dualism, are taken up in the appropriate chapters, in this case the work and health chapters, Chapters 8 and 10, respectively. Like so much else in this book, however, they have implications for many other fields as well. To paraphrase Ivan Illich, when he explained why he singled out education, transportation, and then the medical

profession for his critique of technology and disempow-
erment, I might just as well have chosen to write about
the post office (or politics for that matter).[3]

Because rigidly following set rules and being mindful are, by definition, incompatible, this book will not
offer prescriptions. Many who have read the manuscript
in earlier stages or collaborated with me on the research
have found, as I have, that thinking about mindfulness
and mindlessness has altered their views of the world.
Some have found it easier to take risks and to welcome
change, or have felt less fearful of failure; others have
felt control where they once felt helpless, or freer where
they once felt confined. I hope that readers will enjoy
the glimpses into our research, question its conclusions
mindfully, and test the implications in their own lives

PART ONE

Mindlessness

CHAPTER 2

*

When the Light's On and Nobody's Home

*

Out of time we cut "days" and "nights," "summers" and "winters." We say *what* each part of the sensible continuum is, and all these abstract *whats* are concepts.

The intellectual life of man consists almost wholly in his substitution of a conceptual order for the perceptual order in which his experience originally comes.
WILLIAM JAMES, "The World We Live In"

*

Imagine that it's two o'clock in the morning. Your doorbell rings; you get up, startled, and make your way downstairs. You open the door and see a man standing before you. He wears two diamond rings and a fur coat, and there's a Rolls Royce behind him. He's sorry to wake you at this ridiculous hour, he tells you, but he's in the middle of a scavenger hunt. His ex-wife is in the same contest, which makes it very important to him that he win. He needs a piece of wood about three feet by seven feet. Can you help him? In order to make it worthwhile he'll give you $10,000. You believe him. He's obviously rich. And so you say to yourself, how in the world can I get this piece of wood for him? You think of the lumber yard; you don't know who owns the lumber yard; in fact you're not even sure where the lumber yard is. It would be closed at two o'clock in the morning anyway. You struggle but you can't come up with anything. Reluctantly, you tell him, "Gee, I'm sorry."

The next day, when passing a construction site near a friend's house, you see a piece of wood that's just about the right size, three feet by seven feet—a door. You could have just taken a door off its hinges and given it to him, for $10,000.

Why on earth, you say to yourself, didn't it occur to you to do that? It didn't occur to you because yesterday your door was not a piece of wood. The seven-by-three foot piece of wood was hidden from you, stuck in the category called "door."

This kind of mindlessness, which usually takes more humdrum forms—"Why didn't I think of Susan? She can unclog sinks"—could be called "entrapment by category." It is one of three definitions that can help us understand the nature of mindlessness. The other two, which we will also explain, are automatic behavior and acting from a single perspective.

Trapped by Categories

We experience the world by creating categories and making distinctions among them. "This is a Chinese, not a Japanese, vase." "No, he's only a freshman." "The white orchids are endangered." "She's his boss now." In this way, we make a picture of the world, and of ourselves. Without categories the world might seem to escape us. Tibetan Buddhists call this habit of mind "The Lord of Speech":

We adopt sets of categories which serve as ways of managing phenomena. The most fully developed products of this tendency are ideologies, the systems of ideas that rationalize, justify and sanctify our lives. Nationalism, communism, existentialism, Christianity, Buddhism—all provide us with identities, rules of action, and interpretations of how and why things happen as they do.[1]

The creation of new categories, as we will see throughout this book, is a mindful activity. Mindlessness sets in when we rely too rigidly on categories and distinctions created in the past (masculine/feminine, old/young, success/failure). Once distinctions are created, they take on a life of their own. Consider: (1) First there was earth. (2) Then there was land, sea, and sky. (3) Then there were countries. (4) Then there was Germany. (5) Now there is East Germany versus West Germany. The categories we make gather momentum and are very hard to overthrow. We build our own and our shared realities and then we become victims of them—blind to the fact that they are constructs, ideas.

If we look back at the categories of an earlier age, once firmly established, it is easier to see why new ones might become necessary. The Argentinean writer Jorge Luis Borges quotes from an ancient Chinese encyclopedia in which the animals are classified as "(a) belonging to the Emperor, (b) embalmed, (c) tame, (d) suckling pigs, (e) sirens, (f) stray dogs, (g) included in the present classification, (h) frenzied, (i) innumerable, (j) drawn with a very fine camel brush, (k) et cetera, (l) having just broken the water pitcher, (m) that from a long way off look like flies."[2] To be mindless is to be trapped in a rigid world in which certain creatures always belong to the Emperor, Christianity is always good, certain people are forever untouchable, and doors are only doors.

Automatic Behavior

Have you ever said "excuse me" to a store mannequin or written a check in January with the previous year's date? When in this mode, we take in and use limited signals from the world around us (the female form, the familiar face of the check) without letting other signals (the motionless pose, a calendar) penetrate as well.

Once, in a small department store, I gave a cashier a new credit card. Noticing that I hadn't signed it, she handed it back to me to sign. Then she took my card, passed it through her machine, handed me the resulting form, and asked me to sign it. I did as I was told. The cashier then held the form next to the newly signed card to see if the signatures matched.

Modern psychology has not paid much attention to how much complicated action may be performed automatically, yet as early as 1896 Leon Solomons and Gertrude Stein looked into this question. (This was *the* Gertrude Stein who, from 1893 to 1898, was a graduate student in experimental psychology at Harvard University, working under William James.) They studied what was then called "double personalities" and which later came to be known as "split personalities," and proposed that the mindless performance of the second personality was essentially similar to that of ordinary people. Ordinary people also engage in a great deal of complex behavior without consciously paying attention to it. Solomons and Stein conducted several experiments in which they were their own subjects, demonstrating that both writing and reading could be done automatically. They succeeded in writing English words while they were otherwise caught up in reading an absorbing story. With much practice, they were even able to take dictation automatically while reading. Afterward, they were completely unable to recall the words they had written but were nevertheless quite certain they had written something. To show that reading could take place automatically, the subject read aloud from a book while a captivating story was read to him or her. Again they found that, after a lot of practice, they could read aloud unhampered while giving full attention to the story being read to them.

Solomons and Stein concluded that a vast number

of actions that we think of as intelligent, such as reading and writing, can be done quite automatically: "We have shown a general tendency on the part of normal people, to *act*, without any express desire or conscious volition, in a manner in general accord with the *previous habits* of the person."[3]

An experiment I conducted in 1978 with fellow psychologists Benzion Chanowitz and Arthur Blank explored this kind of mindlessness.[4] Our setting was the Graduate Center at the City University of New York. We approached people using a copying machine and asked whether they would let us copy something then and there. We gave reasons that were either sound or senseless. An identical response to both sound and senseless requests would show that our subjects were not thinking about what was being said. We made one of three requests: "Excuse me, may I use the Xerox machine?"; "Excuse me, may I use the Xerox machine because I want to make copies?"; "Excuse me, may I use the Xerox machine because I'm in a rush?"

The first and second requests are the same in *content*—What else would one do with a copying machine except make copies? Therefore if people were considering what was actually being said, the first two requests should be equally effective. Structurally, however, they are different. The redundant request ("Excuse me, may I use the Xerox machine because I want to make copies?") is more similar to the last one ("Excuse me, may I use the Xerox machine because I'm in a rush?") in that both state the request and give a reason. If people comply with the last two requests in equal numbers, this implies attention to structure rather than conscious attention to content. That, in fact, was just what we found. There was more compliance when a reason was given—whether the reason sounded legitimate or silly. People responded mindlessly to the familiar framework rather than mindfully attending to the content.

Of course, there are limits to this. If someone asked for a very large favor or if the excuse were unusually absurd ("because an elephant is after me"), the individual would be likely to think about what was said. It is not that people don't hear the request the rest of the time; they simply don't think about it actively.

In a similar experiment, we sent an interdepartmental memo around some university offices. The message either requested or demanded the return of the memo to a designated room—and that was all it said.[5] ("Please return this immediately to Room 247," or "This memo is to be returned to Room 247.") Anyone who read such a memo mindfully would ask, "If whoever sent the memo wanted it, why did he or she send it?" and therefore would not return the memo. Half of the memos were designed to look exactly like those usually sent between departments. The other half were made to look in some way different. When the memo looked like those they were used to, 90 percent of the recipients actually returned it. When the memo looked different, 60 percent returned it.

When I was discussing these studies at a university colloquium, a member of the audience told me about a little con game that operated along the same lines. Someone placed an ad in a Los Angeles newspaper that read, "It's not too late to send $1 to _____," and gave the person's own name and address. The reader was promised nothing in return. Many people replied, enclosing a dollar. The person who wrote the ad apparently earned a good sum.

The automatic behavior in evidence in these examples has much in common with habit.[6] Habit, or the tendency to keep on with behavior that has been repeated over time, naturally implies mindlessness. However, as we will see in the following chapter, mindless behavior can arise without a long history of repetition, almost instantaneously, in fact.

Acting from a Single Perspective

So often in our lives, we act as though there were only one set of rules. For instance, in cooking we tend to follow recipes with dutiful precision. We add ingredients as though by official decree. If the recipe calls for a pinch of salt and four pinches fall in, panic strikes, as though the bowl might now explode. Thinking of a recipe only as a rule, we often do not consider how people's tastes vary, or what fun it might be to make up a new dish.

The first experiment I conducted in graduate school explored this problem of the single perspective. It was a pilot study to examine the effectiveness of different requests for help. A fellow investigator stood on a busy sidewalk and told people passing by that she had sprained her knee and needed help. If someone stopped she asked him or her to get an Ace bandage from the nearby drugstore. I stood inside the store and listened while the helpful person gave the request to the pharmacist, who had agreed earlier to say that he was out of Ace bandages. After being told this, not one subject, out of the twenty-five we studied, thought to ask if the pharmacist could recommend something else. People left the drugstore and returned empty-handed to the "victim" and told her the news. We speculated that had she asked for less specific help, she might have received it. But, acting on the single thought that a sprained knee needs an Ace bandage, no one tried to find other kinds of help.

As a little test of how a narrow perspective can dominate our thinking, read the following sentence:

FINAL FOLIOS SEEM TO RESULT FROM YEARS OF DUTIFUL STUDY OF TEXTS ALONG WITH YEARS OF SCIENTIFIC EXPERIENCE.

Now count how many F's there are, reading only once more through the sentence.

If you find fewer than there actually are (the answer is given in the notes[7]), your counting was probably influenced by the fact that the first two words in the sentence begin with F. In counting, your mind would tend to cling to this clue, or single perspective, and miss some of the F's hidden within and at the end of words.

Highly specific instructions such as these or the

request for an Ace bandage encourage mindlessness. Once we let them in, our minds snap shut like a clam on ice and do not let in new signals. In the next chapter we'll take a look at some of the reasons we get stuck in a rigid, closed-off state of mind.

CHAPTER 3

*

The Roots of Mindlessness

We know that the first step towards the intellectual
mastery of the world in which we live is the discovery
of general principles, rules and laws which bring order
into chaos. By such mental operations we simplify the
world of phenomena, but we cannot avoid falsifying it
in doing so, especially when we are dealing with processes of development and change.
SIGMUND FREUD, "Analysis Terminable and
Interminable"

*

As Freud points out, the rules and laws by which we
first attempt to understand the world later lead to a
falsified view. Nevertheless, we then tend to cling to
these rules and the categories we construct from them,
in a mindless manner. Among the reasons for this are
repetition, practice, and a more subtle and powerful
effect that psychologists call premature cognitive commitment. In this chapter we will examine each of these
processes in turn, as well as some of the mindsets that
tend to perpetuate them.

The Mindless "Expert"

Anyone who is able to knit while watching TV, or listen to the radio while driving, knows how learned tasks drop out of mind. As we repeat a task over and over again and become better at it, the individual parts of the task move out of our consciousness. Eventually, we come to assume that we *can* do the task although we no longer know *how* we do it. In fact, questioning the process can have surprising results. If something or someone makes us question our competence on a task that we know moderately well but is *not* overlearned in this way, we can search our minds for the steps of the task and find them. We can then conclude that we are *not* incompetent. However, if we know a task so well that we can perform it "expertly" (mindlessly), these steps may no longer be consciously available and we may doubt our competence.

In my office there was once a very fast typist— demonically fast, in fact—who was also able to read over and retain what he was typing. He had built up these advanced skills over time. One day while he was happily typing away, I asked him if he could teach me to do what he did. As he began to take apart each skill, his quick fingers slowed way down and so did his memory for how and what he typed. Becoming conscious or mindful incapacitated him.

To learn whether this kind of mindlessness is an ingredient in other kinds of behavior, my colleague Cynthia Weinman and I conducted an experiment in extemporaneous speaking.[1] We asked people in an unemployment line in Boston to serve as our subjects for a "linguistic study of voice quality." (No one in this city is safe from our ideas.) Those who agreed were asked to talk into our tape recorder. Half were asked to speak about why it was difficult to find a job in Boston. The other half were asked to speak about finding a job in Alaska—presumably an issue to which they had not given much thought. Half of each of these two groups were asked to think about their given topic first. The results were clear-cut. Subjects were much more fluent when they were discussing a novel issue after being given time to think about it first *or* when they spoke about a familiar topic right away, with no time to think about it. Thinking about a very familiar topic disrupted their performance.

Repetition can lead to mindlessness in almost any profession. If you asked an experienced and a novice typist to type a paragraph without the usual spaces separating words, "acrossthesealives, etc.," it is likely that the person with less experience will have an edge. When any much-repeated task is slightly modified in an unusual way, the novice may do better.

A familiar structure or rhythm helps lead to mental laziness, acting as a signal that there is no need to pay attention. The rhythm of the familiar lulls us into mindlessness:

Q. What do we call the tree that grows from acorns?
A. Oak.
Q. What do we call a funny story?
A. Joke.
Q. What do we call the sound made by a frog?

A. Croak.
Q. What do we call the white of an egg?
A. Yolk. (*sic!*)[2]

Children love these word traps for mindlessness. The game called "Giant Step" or "Mother May I" is built around the pitfalls of repetition.

The Sacrilegious Poodle

Another way that we become mindless is by forming a mindset when we first encounter something and then clinging to it when we reencounter that same thing. Because such mindsets form before we do much reflection, we call them *premature cognitive commitments*. When we accept an impression or a piece of information at face value, with no reason to think critically about it, perhaps because it seems irrelevant, that impression settles unobtrusively into our minds until a similar signal from the outside world—such as sight or smell or sound—calls it up again. At that next time it may no longer be irrelevant, but most of us don't reconsider what we mindlessly accepted earlier. Such mindsets, especially those formed in childhood, are premature because we cannot know in advance the possible future uses a piece of information may serve. The mindless individual is *committed* to one predetermined use of the information, and other possible uses or applications are not explored.

Moisten your mouth with your saliva—the back

of your teeth, the tip of your tongue, and so on. It should feel pleasant. Now spit some saliva into a clean glass. Finally, sip a small bit of this liquid back into your mouth. Disgusting, isn't it? Why? For a number of reasons, we learned years ago that spitting is nasty. Even when there is no sensible reason for the body to feel repelled, the old mindset prevails.

An extreme version of these early mindsets was given to me by a friend who had grown up in a small, predominantly Polish Catholic steel- and coal-mining town. Being one of the few non-Catholic members of the community she was able, indeed more or less forced, to stand on the outside and observe the ordinary peculiarities of the larger community. The priest was a familiar sight in the town, usually accompanied by his splendid gray poodle. This large dog was well trained and often could be seen carrying a newspaper or the priest's umbrella. On this particular Sunday the good Father walked along, enjoying the scenery, on his way home from Mass. His dog walked by his side, also happy and serene, carrying the priest's prayer book in his mouth just as he had carried the paper on other days of the week. The dog, a gentle creature, did no harm to the book. But the nuns who watched the priest and his poodle criticized him fiercely. In their eyes, a dog's mouth was foul, and the book of prayer was being defiled. Despite the piety and good reputation of the priest, and the gentleness of the poodle, all the nuns could see was God in the mouth of a dog.

Benzion Chanowitz and I found a way to test the effects of premature cognitive commitment.[3] For this

experiment, we created a "disease," a perceptual disorder we called *chromosynthosis*. Chromosynthosis was described as a hearing problem in which the affected
individuals have difficulty distinguishing between certain sounds. Our research participants were told they
were going to be tested to determine whether they had
this disorder. They were given booklets that described
the symptoms of chromosynthosis. The disorder, the
booklets said, was like color blindness in that you could
have it without knowing it. The point of the study was
to find out whether, if people learned about this imaginary disorder mindlessly, the impression they formed
would affect their performance on a given task.

We did not give all the participants the same booklets. Some booklets said that 80 percent of the population had the disorder, the implication being that they
stood a good chance of having it. For these subjects,
the information in the booklet was likely to appear
relevant. We asked them to think about how they could
help themselves, should they be found to suffer from
chromosynthosis. For another group, the booklets said
that only 10 percent of the population had the disorder,
the implication being that they were unlikely to have
it. We did not ask them to reflect on how they would
handle the problem, and there appeared to be no strong
reason for them to spend time thinking about it.[4]

All the subjects were then asked to listen to two
sixty-second recordings of natural conversation and to
mark down the number of "a" sounds that they heard.
After scoring their own performances, all the participants discovered that they had chromosynthosis. We

then gave follow-up tests requiring specific abilities that the booklets said are lacking in people with the disorder.

We found that subjects who were given information about a disease that was apparently irrelevant to them became more vulnerable to the symptoms. Once they discovered that they had the disorder they performed poorly. On the follow-up tests they performed only half as well as those comparison subjects who had assumed all along that they might have the disorder and thus had reason to reflect on how to compensate for it. These results confirmed our hypothesis: The way we first take in information (that is, mindfully or mindlessly) determines how we will use it later. In later chapters we will explore this kind of premature cognitive commitment as it relates to aging and such conditions as alcoholism.

Mindlessness and the Unconscious

Certain kinds of mindless acts, such as slips of the tongue, are attributed to the "unconscious." Because the pervasive mindlessness that we are talking about here has other origins, it is important to digress briefly and consider a few of the differences. Unconscious processes, as defined by Freud (or, centuries earlier, by Plato and Buddhist and Hindu philosophers), are considered both dynamic and inaccessible. They are dynamic in that they continuously affect our conscious lives yet, without extreme effort such as is required in psychoanalysis or various spiritual disciplines, we cannot recognize or change their influence.

It is by no means impossible for the product of unconscious activity to pierce into consciousness, but a certain amount of exertion is needed for this task. When we try to do it in ourselves, we become aware of a distinct feeling of *repulsion* which must be overcome, and when we produce it in a patient we get the most unquestionable sign of what we call *resistance* to it. So we learn that the unconscious idea is excluded from consciousness by living forces which oppose themselves to its reception, while they do not object to other ideas, the (pre)conscious ones.[5]

As Freud points out here, for unconscious thoughts there is *motivated-not-knowing*. These unacceptable thoughts and desires may sneak out sideways in dreams, giving us a clue that there is an unconscious influence in our lives, but otherwise they are unavailable to us. "In all of us," wrote Plato, "even in good men, there is a lawless wild beast nature which peers out in sleep." "Reasoning" and "shame" become suspended and the "beast within us . . . goes forth to satisfy his desires."[6]

Mindlessness is not nearly so dramatic a concept. Our motives are not involved. When we learn something mindlessly, it does not occur to us to think about it later, irrespective of whether such thoughts would be acceptable to us. Thus, while ideas in the unconscious are unavailable from the start, mindless ideas were once potentially accessible for mindful processing.

One need not work through deep-seated personal conflict to make conscious those thoughts that are mindlessly processed. However, such thoughts will not, on their own, occur to the person for reconsideration. In that way, they too are inaccessible. But if we are offered a new use for a door or a new view of old age, we can erase the old mindsets without difficulty.

Belief in Limited Resources

One of the main reasons we may become entrapped by the absolute categories we create (or are given by someone else) rather than accept the world as dynamic and continuous is because we believe that resources are limited. If there are clear and stable categories, then we can make rules by which to dole out these resources. If resources weren't so limited, or if these limits were greatly exaggerated, the categories wouldn't need to be so rigid.

Placements in college, for example, are seen as limited. If we act as though intelligence is a single, fixed quality, then we can decide categorically who should go to college on the basis of intelligence. As soon as we realize that intelligence, like everything else, is simultaneously many things, each of which grows and fades depending on context, then we cannot use it to decide categorically who should go and who shouldn't. One could even make matters more confusing and argue that if placements were limited, perhaps the so-called less intelligent should go because they need the education more. Such reasoning would surely lead those denied college admission to recognize that, as with elementary school, there is no intrinsic reason for college education to be limited in availability.

Consider a different example: a divorcing couple with a child. Who will "get" the child? This may be the wrong question. What is actually at stake? Is it the physical presence of the child that the parents want, or is it a certain relationship with the child? Is it the child's body or the child's unlimited love they seek? Or is it a way to get back at each other for whatever hurt was experienced in their relationship? A mindful consideration of what is actually being sought might show that there is enough of the so-called limited resource to go around. A child's love is not a zero-sum commodity. Two people can love and be loved by a child. Feelings are not a limited resource, yet we often don't recognize this because we focus on elements of them that do appear limited.

As long as people cling to a narrow belief in limited resources, those who are fortunate enough to win by the arbitrary (but rigid) rules that are set up, such as SAT scores, have a stake in maintaining the status quo. Those who are not getting what they want, however, might pause to consider that they may be part of someone else's costly construction of reality.

In discussions of limited resources, someone will always bring up money. Money, in most people's experience, is limited. But even here, is money the issue? Why is rich better? Rich people have power, respect, time to play, places they can go to enjoy themselves. They can buy faster cars and finer foods. And so on.

After certain basic human needs are met, isn't what is being sought a state of mind?

If we examine what is behind our desires, we can usually get what we want without compromising: love, caring, confidence, respectability, excitement. Compromising is necessary only if what we want is in short supply. If the valuable things in life were not perceived to be limited, we might not cling so steadfastly to our rigid categories, and we would be more likely to loosen these categorical distinctions once we realize that they have been of our own making, mindlessly entrapping us.

Natural resources surely appear limited. Consider coal, for example, which is deemed a resource because of the function it serves to produce heat. While the amount of coal available may be in limited supply, other ways of serving that function are numerous. Such resources may ultimately be limited, but they are certainly less so than believed by most people.

When we think of resources being limited, we often think of our own abilities. Here, too, our notion of limits may inhibit us. We may push ourselves to what we believe are our limits, in swimming, public speaking, or mathematics. However, whether they are true limits is not determinable.[7]

It may be in our best interest to proceed as though these and other abilities might be improved upon, so that at least we will not be deterred by false limits. It was once assumed that humans could not run the mile in fewer than five minutes. In 1922 it was said to be "humanly impossible" to run the mile in less than four minutes. In 1952 that limit was broken by Roger Bannister. Each time a record is broken, the supposed limit is extended. Yet the notion of limits persists.

A curious example of apparent limits being transcended is known as the Coolidge Effect. Observers of rats, hamsters, cats, sheep, and other animals have long noted that when a male animal's sexual appetite is sated, and he has finished copulating, he needs a rest period. If a new female of the species is brought in, however, he will immediately find the energy to resume mating.[8]

Camp counselors know all about the subjective nature of limits. Every summer, a counselor friend of mine in New Hampshire takes six twelve-year-old boys for a climb up a small peak called Mount Chocorua. After many years, he knows the mountain and knows just when energy will flag. When a breathless camper asks, "How much longer?" he answers that he isn't sure. The last stretch of the climb is a ridge from which the summit can be seen, all bare rock and jagged against the sky. It was here that the Indian Chief Chocorua was chased at gunpoint by the white men who wanted his people's land.

When the sweaty campers reach this ridge, they often flop down and take off their heavy knapsacks. Just at this point, the counselor catches their attention with the story of Chief Chocorua. He also explains the particular challenge of this last stretch. Hearing this, the campers see the rest of the climb as a new task. When they reach the rocky summit of Mount Chocorua and feel the wind coming over them from the great Presidential Range of the White Mountains to the north, they are always exultant—and hardly tired. Fatigue, too, can be a premature cognitive commitment.

Entropy and Linear Time as Limiting Mindsets

Associated with a belief in limited resources is the concept of *entropy*, the gradual dissolution or breaking down of an entity or patterns of organization within a closed system. Entropy is an idea that, on the face of it, allows people to feel control: there is more opportunity for involvement in a system that wears down over time—where things successively get worse—than in one where things stay the same or get better and better on their own. The notion of entropy gives rise to an image of the universe as a great machine that is running down. Such an image, which many of us have accepted without ever really thinking about it, may also be an unfortunate and unnecessary mindset that narrows our sense of what is possible. An alternate view of the world, for instance, one that recognizes how much of our reality is socially constructed, may actually afford more personal control.

A belief in fixed limits is not compatible with the views of many physicists. James Jeans and Sir Arthur Eddington, for example, believed the universe is best described as a great idea. It is there to be acted upon. As soon as any system seems almost complete something new, now unforeseen, will be discovered.

A related notion that may also limit us unnecessarily is the linear view of time. If we consider how notions of time have shifted across cultures and throughout history, it might be easier for us to question this restrictive view.

In some cultures, time is treated as a universal present. In the Trobriand Islands, off the coast of Papua New Guinea, people do not think of the past as a previous phase of present time. The Hopi Indians, like the Trobrianders, do not hold our linear concept of time, though they have many concepts (becoming, imaginary versus real) that fulfill similar functions. John Edward Orme speculates that in primitive times, people held time to be an "all at once" phenomenon.[9] Polynesians are careful to deny the novelty of any adventure. Rather, they believe that they are only repeating the voyage of a mythical explorer.

Another view of time is one that sees it as cyclical. Pythagoras believed that every detail of time would be repeated. The concept of reincarnation, held by many religions in the Far East, implies a cyclical view. Nietzsche also argued that the universe is cyclical, that events may be repeated. From this point of view, precognition is not so much a glimpse into the future as seeing what happened in the past, in another cycle. In a cyclic model of time, the future and past are indistinguishable.

Even in a one-dimensional model of time, movement may not be exclusively unidirectional. The future may be as capable of "causing" the present as is the past. What should I study now for the exam I'm taking later? St. Augustine said, "The present, therefore, has several dimensions . . . the present of things past, the present of things present, and the present of things future."

Kant conceived of time as a means of organizing perception—not as something "given" by the world, nor as something "projected" on it. From this concept he developed the "synthetic a priori" in mathematics: truth we can know about the world without looking at the world.

Changing one's mindset about time may be more than an intellectual exercise. For example, in Chapter 10, which looks at mindfulness and health, we question the belief that healing always takes a fixed amount of time. Alternative views of time make such questioning seem more plausible. Actually, certainty with respect to the meaning of time seems absurd. According to an eminent physicist, Ernst Mach, "It is utterly beyond our power to measure things in time. Quite the contrary, time is an abstraction, at which we arrive by means of the change of things."[10]

Education for Outcome

A very different, but not incompatible, explanation for why we become mindless has to do with our early education. From kindergarten on, the focus of schooling is usually on goals rather than on the process by which they are achieved. This single-minded pursuit of one outcome or another, from tying shoelaces to getting into Harvard, makes it difficult to have a mindful attitude about life.

When children start a new activity with an outcome orientation, questions of "Can I?" or "What if I can't do it?" are likely to predominate, creating an anxious preoccupation with success or failure rather than drawing on the child's natural, exuberant desire to explore. Instead of enjoying the color of the crayon, the designs on the paper, and a variety of possible shapes along the way, the child sets about writing a "correct" letter A.

Throughout our lives, an outcome orientation in social situations can induce mindlessness. If we think we know how to handle a situation, we don't feel a need to pay attention. If we respond to the situation as very familiar (a result, for example, of overlearning), we notice only the minimal cues necessary to carry out the proper scenario. If, on the other hand, the situation is strange, we might be so preoccupied with thoughts of failure ("What if I make a fool of myself?") that we miss nuances of our own and others' behavior. In this sense, we are mindless with respect to the immediate situation, although we may be thinking quite actively about outcome-related issues.

In contrast, a process orientation, which we will explore when we look at creativity in Chapter 7, asks "How do I do it?" instead of "Can I do it?" and thus directs attention toward defining the steps that are necessary on the way. This orientation can be characterized in terms of the guiding principle that *there are no failures, only ineffective solutions.*

In computer programming classes for children, a major activity is "bug fixing"—figuring out new solutions, instead of getting hung up on a particular one that didn't work. Provisional goals are subject to continual revision. The process-oriented person is less likely to be caught off-guard if circumstances change.

The style of education that concentrates on outcomes generally also presents facts unconditionally. This approach encourages mindlessness. If something is presented as an accepted truth, alternative ways of thinking do not even come up for consideration. Such a single-minded way of viewing the world can generalize to virtually everything we do. By teaching absolutes we pass our culture from one generation to the next. It brings stability. But as we will see, the cost may be high.

The Power of Context

The way we behave in any situation has a lot to do with the context. We whisper in hospitals and become anxious in police stations, sad in cemeteries, docile in schools, and jovial at parties. Contexts control our behavior, and our mindsets determine how we interpret each context.

Many of the contexts that affect us most deeply are learned in childhood. For instance, our early visual exposure to the world may actually shape what we later see. A controversial study of Euro-Canadians brought up in urban settings where buildings surround them with right angles, and with Cree Indians raised near tents and lodges that have many shapes and angles, suggested that the effects of early visual context may be lasting. In adulthood, right angles could be seen better than other line orientations by the Euro-Canadians. At the same time, they seemed to have less visual acuity for oblique orientations than the Cree. From the beginning, the Cree have a different mental landscape which may allow them to take in a greater variety of visual cues.[11]

A classic example of the power of context is the tale of the ugly duckling. When he came out of his egg, the ugly duckling made his first premature cognitive commitment: He looked at the nearest, largest duck and "decided" that she was its mother. Then when his siblings and others tormented him, he made a second premature cognitive commitment—that he was different and, worse still, that he was ugly. So he felt ashamed and alone.

When he ran away from the bullying and teasing, the ugly duckling had a series of adventures. At one point out in a cold marsh a hunting dog came upon him, only to jump over him. For once he was glad about his appearance: "I'm so ugly that even a dog will not eat me." We all know the rest of the story. In a new context—the world of swans—the ugly duckling felt proud and beautiful. His old mindsets floated away as he saw himself next to other long necks and spreading wings.

When we talk about a context, we often make the mistake of believing that it is somehow "out there." If we take words "out of context," we think the context remains on the page. But it doesn't exist there without us. We perceive a relationship between one sentence and the next, just as the cygnet perceived a relationship between himself and the mother duck. A context is a premature cognitive commitment, a mindset.

Context depends on who we are today, who we were yesterday, and from which view we see things. Sometimes these conflict. What would you make of a "Las Vegas Night" run by nuns for the church? If someone started yelling in a hospital because his mother was being mistreated, others would look at him in alarm because yelling does not follow hospital rules. Though there are times in a hospital when it might well be appropriate to stomp and shout, we don't think to do it because of the context.

Shaw's Professor Higgins demonstrated that our perceptions of beauty shift dramatically with context. In the beginning of *Pygmalion*, Eliza Doolittle is a ragged, cockney-accented girl selling flowers in the streets of London. Professor Higgins walks into her life and decides to do her over. Realizing that context is all, he goes to work on Eliza and changes her voice, her diction, her dress, her habits. He puts her in a new setting, the way a jeweler would reset a gem. Eliza becomes a grand hit in London, hailed as a beauty and a princess. The interest of the plot is heightened because the dramatic change in context causes an equally dramatic change in Eliza's self-esteem, indeed in what we would call Eliza "herself."

The location of context in our perceptions was

vividly illustrated in an experiment conducted by psychologists David Holmes and B. Kent Houston.[12] With the permission of the subjects, they administered mild electric shocks to a group of people, half of whom were told to think of electric shocks as new "physiological sensations." Those who thought of the shock in this way were less anxious and had lower pulse rates than those who were not given the prior instructions.

The same situation or stimulus called by a different name is a different stimulus. Roller coasters are fun but bumpy plane rides are not. Imagine the following scene: A woman walking down a country road is suddenly besieged by a swarm of bees. Like most of us would be, she is afraid; her blood pressure rises, her pulse quickens. She may freeze or run in fear. On the other hand, imagine the same woman walking down the same road with a young child by her side. The sight of the bees now signals a very different behavior. In this context, she boldly protects the child instead of becoming afraid. The same bees have become a different stimulus.

Context can determine value. A postal clerk, so a report in the *Boston Globe* would have us believe, created public acceptance of the disfavored Susan B. Anthony dollar coin simply by announcing "limit two per customer."[13] For retailers, this is an old story.

Context can be an influence even when we are trying to make the most precise and specific judgments. In a study by Donald Brown, subjects were asked to lift various weights and judge them as light, medium, heavy, or very heavy.[14] In some cases Brown introduced an anchor (another weight). The hypothesis was that judged weight would vary according to how the anchor weight differed from the weight being judged. This is just what Brown found. The introduction of a heavy anchor weight made the same weight feel lighter than it had before the anchor was introduced.

Brown added an interesting variation. Some subjects were asked to make matters easier for the experimenter by picking up and moving the tray on which the weights sat. If weights were influenced by other weights, would subjects be influenced by the weight of the tray as well? Though the tray was not perceived as part of the task, one would think it existed in some absolute way independent of the perceiver's psychology. One would expect that its weight would influence the subject despite the fact that it was not officially part of the experiment. However, if context rather than so-called physical reality determines our experiences of stimuli, then the tray should have no influence.

The results of this ingenious experiment showed that judgment of weight was *not* influenced by the weight of the tray. It was as if subjects entered the context of the experiment and were influenced by the various weights and then took themselves out of that context to remove the tray. They then placed themselves back in the weight-judging situation. In a sense, for them the tray had no weight.

It has long been known that values create a context that influences sense perceptions. In 1948, Leo Postman, Jerome Bruner, and Eliot McGinnies used a machine called a tachistoscope to flash words very quickly on a screen.[15] These words were associated with various values. For example, subjects were shown political words such as *govern*, *citizen*, and *politics*; religious words such as *prayer*, *sacred*, and *worship*; and aesthetic words such as *poetry*, *artist*, and *beauty*. In all, the words represented six different values measured by the Allport-Vernon Study of Values.[16] Words were shown to subjects in random order. Despite the fact that the chosen words were equally familiar, the speed with which subjects recognized the words varied as a consequence of the subjects' values, as measured by the same Allport-Vernon Scale given earlier to subjects. The higher a subject's score on a particular value, the more quickly he or she recognized the word. Politically oriented subjects, for example, recognized political words sooner than the artistically oriented. The context created by the subjects' values appeared to affect their visual ability.

This power of context over our reactions and interpretations also makes us susceptible to what we may call *context confusion*. Here people confuse the context controlling the behavior of another person with the context determining their own behavior. Most people typically assume that other peoples' motives and intentions are the same as theirs, although the same behavior may have very different meanings. If I am out running and see someone walking briskly, I assume she is trying to exercise and would run if only she could. Yet, she might have deliberately chosen to get her exercise from walking, which she enjoys. Walking and running are mutually exclusive, as is often the case with context confused behavior: *To be accomplishing one, you are necessarily not accomplishing the other.* If society values running, however, over time this woman may come to see herself as "not running" rather than as electing to walk. Forgetting the pleasure she felt in walking, she might come to see herself as an incompetent runner.

This context confusion often happens with "out" groups when we or they scrutinize their behavior. To their detriment, they tend to be evaluated by criteria that are irrelevant to their initial intentions and goals. They may be unaware of why they first engaged in a particular action, and thus can be persuaded by the larger, more powerful group that they are behaving incompetently. The "in" group has unwittingly redefined the context of the "out" group members' behavior. We will examine this further in Chapter 9 when we look at prejudice.

The various causes of mindlessness that we have just discussed—repetition, premature cognitive commitment, belief in limited resources, the notion of linear time, education for outcome, and the powerful influence of context—influence each day of our lives. Before we discuss how to counteract them with a mindful outlook, we will take a look at just what we lose when we act mindlessly.

CHAPTER 4

*

The Costs of Mindlessness

Three older women were sitting on a park bench. One
groaned. Her friend, sitting next to her, gave a sigh.
The third looked at both of them and said, "I thought
we weren't going to talk about the children."

*

The grooves of mindlessness run deep. We know our
scripts by heart. In the routine of daily life we do not
notice what we are doing unless there is a problem.
Locking ourselves out of a car or throwing socks in the
garbage instead of the laundry basket jolts us awake.
William James tells a story of starting to get ready for
a dinner party, undressing, washing, and then climbing
into bed. Two routines that begin the same way got
confused, and he mindlessly followed the more familiar
one.

Closer to home, a friend told me a nice three-
generation story of mindlessness. One day a woman
was about to cook a roast. Before putting it in the pot,
she cut off a small slice. When asked why she did this,

she paused, became a little embarrassed, and said she did it because her mother had always done the same thing when she cooked a roast. Her own curiosity aroused, she telephoned her mother to ask why she always cut off a little slice before cooking her roast. The mother's answer was the same: "Because that's the way my mother did it." Finally, in need of a more helpful answer, she asked her grandmother why she always cut off a little slice before cooking a roast. Without hesitating, her grandmother replied, "Because that's the only way it would fit in my pot."

The consequences of mindlessness range from the trivial to the catastrophic. At the dire extreme is a young man who went to a party at a grand estate in the New Hampshire woods. Late in the evening he went outside to the garden with a young woman. Through the darkness he saw a big swimming pool. Feeling playful, he tore off most of his clothes, gave a Tarzan yell, banged his chest, and dove off the diving board—onto solid concrete. The young man broke his neck.

Between trivia and tragedy is a wide range of less obvious but nevertheless serious effects of mindlessness. These include an inhibiting self-image, unintended cruelty, loss of control, and stunted potential.

A Narrow Self-Image

A single-minded self-image leaves both individuals and corporations dangerously vulnerable. Perhaps a housewife, for example, defines herself narrowly in everything she does. When meeting people, she may introduce herself as "So and so's wife." She sees herself as managing "his house," buying herself clothes "he likes," and cooking for him. Although she may very well be happy in this rigid role, what would happen if her husband decided to pack his bags and leave? Would she be able to function when the rules changed? Any "housewife" fills many other roles: daughter, sister, friend, carpenter, amateur painter, and so on. By mindfully becoming aware of these distinctions, she would be less vulnerable to the loss. If she expanded her definition of herself in terms of all these roles, or some subset of them, and something happened to her husband, there would still be great continuity in her life.

The costs of a single-minded self-image are equally severe for a corporation. Management can define a business as serving certain markets and become entrapped by its own categories. In a classic paper written for the *Harvard Business Review* in 1975, entitled "Marketing Myopia," Theodore Levitt[1] wrote:

The railroads did not stop growing because the need for passenger and freight transportation declined. That grew. The railroads are in trouble today not because the need was filled by others (cars, trucks, airplanes, even telephones), but because it was *not* filled by the railroads themselves. They let others take customers away from them because they *assumed themselves to be in the railroad business rather than in the transportation business.* [Italics added.]

The advantage of an evolving, multifaceted self- or corporate image will be seen in all the chapters that follow.

Our tendency to focus on outcome, which we discussed in the last chapter, also narrows our self-image. When we envy other people's assets, accomplishments, or characteristics, it is often because we are making a *faulty comparison.* We may be looking at the *results* of their efforts rather than at the *process* they went through on the way. For example, imagine that while talking to a professor in her office, you hear her use a word that you do not understand. You may feel intimidated and stupid. Now imagine that the same professor is sitting at her desk with an open dictionary. You would probably conclude that she knew that strange word because she spends time looking up words, finding them in books she reads, or learning them in some other straightforward way. You too could look up words, if you wanted to. Keeping an eye on process, on the steps anyone must take to become expert, keeps us from disparaging ourselves.

A self-image based on past performance may also inhibit us. Someone who has been able to diet for only two days each time he has tried in the past, or who has not been able to run more than a mile, or who has always had to bring work home on weekends, or who has never been able to figure out how to save money, may assume that this is a permanent part of his or her character. Unless the person's mindset changes, the same lack of success will probably follow these endeavors today or tomorrow. As we saw in the last chapter, however, many of the limits we accept as real are illusory. In a rather simple exercise, two of my colleagues and I instructed one group of subjects to give us as many solutions as they could to a number of ordinary problems (for example: there is no heat, yet you want to stay warm; you want a cold drink but don't have a bottle opener). After these subjects had run out of solutions, we took the largest number anyone had found and asked another group of subjects to give us that many solutions plus five more. No one in the second group had difficulty meeting this goal.[2]

Even people who have achieved a strong sense of competence can find it eroded by mindlessly accepted labels. Before getting married, Ann could balance her checkbook; once married, she let her husband take over the task; now divorced, Ann can't seem to balance her checkbook any longer. Jane is a confident lawyer; she has a baby and takes a leave of absence from her job. Now she wants to go back to work but has lost her confidence.

These rather familiar situations illustrate a phenomenon that we have called *self-induced dependence*. Former graduate student Ann Benevento and I designed a few experiments to see how it develops.[3] We decided to conduct them at the airport, on the assumption that people who travel are likely to be somewhat independent and self-assured. If they could develop self-induced dependence, it was likely to occur in others as well. In the first phase of one of these experiments, the subjects were given arithmetic problems which they could solve with ease. In phase two, we put the subjects in a position likely to lead them to question their competence. We gave some the title of "assistant" and others "boss," and had them all perform tasks in a manner appropriate to their roles. In the third phase, all the subjects returned to the same kind of easy arithmetic problems they had successfully completed in phase one. Those who had been made "assistants" now solved the problems only half as well as they had originally. Though they began participating with equal competence, the labels that they had assumed undermined their performance.

Unintended Cruelty

The costs of mindlessness are not all personal. A look at the famous study on obedience to authority conducted by Stanley Milgram shows one of the ways mindlessness can hurt others.[4] Subjects of this study were asked to participate in research on the effects of punishment on learning. Each time the "learner" did not know the answer to the question, the teacher-subject was supposed to administer an electric shock. The learner didn't really receive any shocks, but the teacher-subjects did not know this. A tape recording played convincing grunts and expressions of discomfort at the apparent shocks. Subjects were asked to increase the shock intensity each time an error was made. Milgram's surprising finding was that 65 percent of these nice, normal people, under instruction from the experimenter/authority, delivered enough current to kill the learner.

This is a much condensed account of a complex and controversial experiment. What is important here is the incremental nature of the actions. Had the experimenter asked subjects to use almost maximum shock intensity from the start for each individual, it is very likely that far fewer subjects would have obeyed. What seems to happen when we take small steps is that, after the first step, we do not think to question our behavior until, by looking back, we can see how far we've unwittingly come. If we cheat somebody out of 50 cents, what's the big deal the next time of cheating him out of $1.00, then $2.00 or $5.00? And so on until something makes us realize that we've behaved poorly. If we fall into a routine rather than make decisions anew each time, we can get mindlessly seduced into activities we wouldn't engage in otherwise.

Mindlessness also allows us to compartmentalize uncomfortable thoughts. When they were little girls of four and five, I took my nieces to feed the ducks at a pond near their house in Connecticut. At first the girls were afraid but then they made friends with these appealing creatures. That evening the family went out for dinner together. I ordered duck. With a look of terror in her eyes, one of my nieces asked, "Aunt Ellie, is that the same . . .?" I quickly changed my order, unable to hold the image of live ducks in my mind while chewing on a cooked one. (Luckily we hadn't visited an entire farm before dinner.)

By locking "pets" into one category and "livestock" into another, we can eat meat without qualms. In this book we will see how much we lose by keeping thoughts in impermeable categories. At our family dinner, however, the ducks bore the cost.

In a number of nursing homes across the country, something called "reality therapy" has become popular but is often misapplied. As part of the program, a member of the staff gets on the public address system at regular times and reports a few of the relevant facts of the day: the temperature outside, the day of the week, political events that have occurred, and the like. To test their grasp of reality, residents are later asked questions such as, "What is the temperature today?" and "What day is it?" Those who cannot answer are deemed confused.

But whose reality is this? To someone indoors all day, the temperature outside is no more than a curiosity. And if every day is experienced as virtually the same, it hardly matters whether today is Tuesday or Thursday, the first or the thirty-first. Seeing "reality" from the staff's single-minded perspective may lead to misreadings of the residents' health or level of awareness and consequently to harmful labeling. The costs of mindless definitions of what is real or normal to both the elderly and the "deviant" are taken up in Chapters 6 and 9.

Loss of Control

Mindlessness limits our control by preventing us from making intelligent choices. Advertisers cater effectively to mindlessness. Once I was walking in midtown Manhattan when my attention was drawn to a large sign in the window of a tourist shop that for the past twenty years or so has been "going out of business."

This sign announced "Candles that burn!" Thinking that special candles make nice presents, I was about to go in and take advantage of this novel offering when it occurred to me that all candles burn.

Even without advertisers conspiring to render us mindless, we often limit our own choices. One important way in which we limit our options is to attribute all our troubles to a single cause. Such mindless attributions narrowly limit the range of solutions we might seek. In research on divorce, psychologist Helen Newman and I found that people who blame the failure of their marriages on their ex-spouses suffer longer than those people who see many possible explanations for their situation.[5]

Similarly, alcoholics who see the cause of their problem as purely genetic seem to give up the control that could help their recovery. When we have a single-minded explanation, we typically don't pay attention to information that runs counter to it. This happens even if the information is given by experienced therapists. In a study of premature cognitive commitments and alcoholism, three colleagues and I found evidence of this.[6] We looked at two kinds of alcoholics: those who in their youth knew only one alcoholic and those who in their youth knew several, each of whom behaved differently from the others. We assumed that this latter group might have a less single-minded view of options. For example, if a child knew only one alcoholic who was loud and cruel, the child might grow up mindlessly assuming that this was the way alcoholics always behaved. If that child later became an alcoholic, it might not occur to him that he could behave differently. However, if the same child had met several other alcoholics with many different personalities, he might be open to a more flexible view of how he might act and of the possibility of change.

First we interviewed forty-two patients attending an alcohol clinic at a general hospital, paying particular attention to their childhood experiences. (The interviewers and therapists were unaware of our hypothesis.) We then compared the results of the interviews with the therapists' evaluations of the patients' degree of improvement. Those who had been successfully helped in therapy virtually always came from the multiple-role-model group. Those who had been exposed to only one model of alcoholism appeared to have developed mindsets so rigid that the options offered by therapy did not seem available to them.

Our tendency to persist mindlessly in using the first model presented to us can be demonstrated in a much simpler form. In a classic set of studies on the effects of *Einstellung*, or mental set, psychologists Abraham Luchins and Edith Hirsch Luchins found that after subjects could perform a mathematical task without thinking, the vast majority kept using the same solutions even when a simpler one became available.[7]

The problem in their experiment consisted of obtaining different amounts of water using three jars of different sizes. For instance, the subject was asked to get 100 quarts of water using Jar A, which holds 21 quarts, Jar B, which holds 127 quarts, and Jar C, which holds 3 quarts. One solution is to start with Jar B and subtract Jar A and then subtract Jar C twice ($127 - 21 - 3 - 3 = 100$). The solution may also be written as Jar B − Jar A − 2 Jar C. Subjects were given a series of problems that all had the same solution.

Once they presumably had this clever answer down cold, they were asked how to get 20 quarts when Jar A = 23, Jar B = 49, and Jar C = 3.

The formula used for the first problem works here also ($49 - 23 - 3 - 3 = 20$). However, there is an easier way to solve the puzzle: Subtract Jar C from Jar A ($23 - 3 = 20$). Luchins and Luchins found that 81 percent of the subjects used the more elaborate formula, apparently oblivious to the simpler alternative. Interestingly, when some subjects were specifically instructed on the answer sheet, "Don't be blind," and not to act "foolishly while solving the subsequent problems," 63 percent of them still performed mindlessly and used the more complicated solution.

Learned Helplessness

A much more pernicious loss of choice and control is brought about by repeated failure. After a number of experiences in which our efforts are futile, many of us will give up. Well-known research by psychologist Martin Seligman and others shows that this *learned helplessness* then generalizes to situations where the person can, in fact, exercise control.[8] Even when solutions are available, a mindless sense of futility prevents a person from reconsidering the situation. The person remains passive in the face of situations that could otherwise be handled without undue difficulty. Past experience determines present reactions and robs the individual of control. If we looked for new aspects of the situations in which we find ourselves, we probably could prevent learned helplessness.

Learned helplessness was originally demonstrated in rats.[9] When placed in ice water, they have no difficulty swimming around for forty to sixty hours. However, if, instead of being put immediately into the water, the rats are held until they stop struggling, something very different happens. Instead of swimming, these rats give up immediately and drown.

Hospitals for the chronically ill often unwittingly teach a similar kind of helplessness. Particularly sad cases have been reported in psychiatric hospitals.[10] In one, the patient lived on what was affectionately called the "hopeless ward." For a time, renovations in the hospital made it necessary for the residents on this ward to be moved temporarily to another ward from which residents usually did get better and return to the community. The patient did well during this time. Once the renovations were completed, however, patients were returned to the hopeless ward. This particular patient died immediately afterward, from no apparent physical cause. The name of the ward had taught him the message written over Dante's Gates of Hell: "Abandon all hope, ye who enter here."

Stunted Potential

William James claimed that almost all of us use only the tiniest fraction of our potential.[11] Only under certain circumstances of constructive stress or in certain states—great love, for example, or religious ardor, or the courage of battle—do we begin to tap the depth and richness of our creative resources, or the tremendous reserves of life energy that lie sleeping within us. Mindlessness, as it diminishes our self-image, narrows our choices, and weds us to single-minded attitudes, has a lot to do with this wasted potential. As I mentioned in the Introduction, this waste has become especially vivid to me because of research I have done with elderly populations. When I've worked with others in trying to make improvements for these people, the main obstacles we had to overcome, both in the older people themselves and in their caretakers, were the premature cognitive commitments about old age that people make in their youth.

Premature cognitive commitments are like photographs in which meaning rather than motion is frozen. When a child hears about stiff, testy old people, the snapshot is processed as is. The child has little stake in the issue. Later, in old age, the grown-up child may not question the image. The original picture can become the foundation for everything learned about old age. Even when corrected, so much else has been built on this foundation that a new attitude is difficult to form.

To test the effects of these early experiences, we compared elderly subjects who in their youth had lived with a grandparent before they were two years old with those who lived with a grandparent only after they were thirteen.[12] We assumed that the grandparents of two-year-olds were likely to have been younger and stronger and to have looked "bigger" than those whose grand-children were thirteen and older. If so, the younger the subjects were during these initial contacts, the more positive would be their premature cognitive commit-ments about age. As a result, they might be expected to adjust more positively to their own old age.

Participants for this study were residents of nurs-ing, convalescent, or retirement homes located in the metropolitan Boston area. Their average age was sev-enty-nine years. We encouraged them to reminisce, and interviewed them about the past to determine whether they had lived with a grandparent when they were growing up and, if so, how old they were when the grandparent moved in.

Later, these participants were independently eval-uated by nurses unaware of our hypothesis. Those whose earliest premature cognitive commitments about aging were more youthful were rated as more alert. They also tended to be seen as more active and more independent.[13]

There may be other possible explanations for these results. Nevertheless, they suggest that we might do well to explore the ways that we have been taught to grow old.

Psychologists tend to follow where novelists have

dared to tread. One of the most harrowing pictures ever drawn of the costs of single-minded, stunted existence is Miss Havisham, in Charles Dickens's *Great Expectations*. For her, ever since the moment she was abandoned on the day of her wedding, mind and time have stopped. We see her through the eyes of the boy Pip, who does not know what misfortune and tragic mindset brought her to this state:

> In an arm-chair, with an elbow resting on the table and her head leaning on that hand, sat the strangest lady I have ever seen, or shall ever see.
> She was dressed in rich material—satins, and lace, and silks—all of white. Her shoes were white. And she had a long white veil dependent from her hair, and she had bridal flowers in her hair, but her hair was white. Some bright jewels sparkled on her neck and on her hands, and some other jewels lay sparkling on the table. . . .
> But I saw that everything within my reach . . . had lost its lustre, and was faded and yellow. I saw that the bride within the bridal dress had withered like the dress, and like the flowers, and had no brightness left but the brightness of her sunken eyes.
> . . . I should have cried out, if I could.[14]

PART TWO

Mindfulness

CHAPTER 5

*

The Nature of Mindfulness

Our life is what our thoughts make it.
MARCUS AURELIUS, *Meditations*

*

When Napoleon invaded Russia, he appeared to the world as a brilliant conquering hero, yet again proving his military genius by daring to march against a giant. But behind the proud banners and eagles, he carried a dangerous mindset, a determination to have Russia, to have Russia no matter what the cost in human life. As Tolstoy describes him in *War and Peace*, Napoleon had no use for alternatives; his determination was absolute.

Opposite Napoleon stood the old Russian bear of a general, Kutuzov, a mellowed veteran who liked his vodka and had a habit of falling asleep at state occasions. An uneven match, or so it would appear.

As Napoleon's army advanced, Kutuzov let his army fall back, and then fall back some more. Napoleon kept coming, deeper into Russia, farther from his supply lines. Finally, as Kutuzov knew would happen, a powerful ally intervened: the Russian winter. The French army found itself fighting the cold, the wind, the snow, and the ice.

When Napoleon at last achieved his single, obsessive goal—Moscow—there was no one there for him to conquer. Everyone had left. The Russians had set their holy city on fire to greet the invader. Once more Kutuzov played the seeming loser.

He knew that an apple should not be picked while it is green. It will fall of itself when ripe, but if plucked unripe the apple is spoilt, the tree is harmed, and your teeth are set on edge. . . . He knew that the beast was wounded as only the whole strength of Russia could have wounded it, but whether it was mortally wounded or not was still an undecided question.[1]

At that moment, when Napoleon had no choice but to retreat—from the burned city, from the winter— the mindful old general attacked. He appealed to Mother Russia, an appeal that Stalin was to use with similar success years later. He appealed to the people to save their land, and that appeal revived all of Russia. The French had everything against them, including the Cossacks, who rode down off the winter steppes. Mother Russia prevailed, just as she would when Hitler was to repeat Napoleon's mistake.

In the character of Kutuzov we can find portrayed the key qualities of a mindful state of being: (1) creation of new categories; (2) openness to new information; and (3) awareness of more than one perspective.

In each case, Napoleon's blind obsession provides a vivid mirror image, a portrait of mindlessness. First of all, Kutuzov was flexible: Evacuating a city would usually fall under the category of defeat, but for him it became the act of setting a trap. Second, his strategy was responsive to the news of Napoleon's advance, while Napoleon did not seem to be taking in information about Kutuzov's moves. Finally, while Napoleon saw his rapid advance and march on Moscow only from the point of view of conquering enemy terrain, Kutuzov could also see that an "invasion" in the context of winter and distance from supplies could be turned into a bitter rout.

Creating New Categories

Just as mindlessness is the rigid reliance on old categories, mindfulness means the continual creation of new ones. Categorizing and recategorizing, labeling and relabeling as one masters the world are processes natural to children. They are an adaptive and inevitable part of surviving in the world.[2] Freud recognized the importance of creation and mastery in childhood:

Should we not look for the first traces of imaginative activity as early as in childhood? The child's best-loved and most intense occupation is with his play or games. Might we not say that every child at play behaves like a creative writer, in that he creates a world of his own, or rather, re-arranges the things of his world in a new way which pleases him?[3]

The child's serious *re-creation* can become the adult's playful *recreation*.

As adults, however, we become reluctant to create new categories. As we saw earlier, our outcome orientation tends to deaden a playful approach. If I asked you to make a list of what you did yesterday, what would you say? Think about it for a moment, then think of what you would say if I offered you money for each item in your answer. Did you list your day in large chunks at first—breakfast, work, lunch, phone calls? Most people will say, for example, that they "ate breakfast" rather than "bit, chewed, and swallowed a piece of toast" and so on, even when offered a reward for a longer list of activities.

Without psychotherapy or a crisis as motivation, the past is rarely recategorized. We might from time to time call upon different episodes from the past to justify a present situation or grievance, but it rarely occurs to us to change the way the events or impressions were initially stored.

For example, take a couple, Alice and Fred, whom you see quite often. Sometimes you hear them fight a bit. You don't pay any attention; don't all couples quarrel? Now you learn that they are getting a divorce. You call to mind all the evidence that explains this outcome. "I knew it, remember how they used to fight? Their fights were vicious." On the other hand, perhaps you hear that they have just celebrated their silver anniversary. "Isn't that nice," you say, "they have such a solid marriage; they hardly ever quarrel and when they do, they always make up so sweetly to each other." While we pick and choose in our store of memories, the original categorizing of what we saw remains the same. In this case, we remember certain behavior as a quarrel. It might come to mind as vicious or playful, but we identify it as a quarrel nonetheless. We don't recategorize the original behavior and say that rather than quarreling, perhaps they were engaging in foreplay or playing a game or practicing a role for a play. Initially, the behavior labeled "quarrel" may have been open to several interpretations. Once it is stored in memory as a quarrel it is not likely to be recategorized, even though it may be called up or left behind to help make some case.

When we make new categories in a mindful way, we pay attention to the situation and the context. If I need someone to help me fix a high ceiling, a tall person might be best. On the other hand, maybe someone who is 5 feet, 2 inches, would be more appropriate—if he is a mountain climber, doesn't mind ladders, and so forth. Breaking down categories of skills to more precise distinctions is a useful approach for a personnel manager. In a very noisy environment a clever programmer who is deaf might be a better job candidate than a person of equal ability but of normal hearing. If sitting for long periods of time is necessary, someone confined to a wheelchair may not mind the sedentery work as much as the next applicant. A simple list of general skills free of context would mask these and many more differentiated distinctions.

Most strong opinions rest on global categories. If we describe someone we dislike intensely, a single statement usually does it. But if, instead, we are forced to describe the person in great detail, eventually there will be some quality we appreciate. This is true of objects or situations as well, and is one way of changing an intolerable situation: We can try to have the good without the bad. Take, for example, someone who hates New England winters. If he lets his thoughts become more differentiated, he may discover that what he really dislikes is feeling restricted by heavy winter clothing. A well-insulated jacket or a better heater in his car might change his outlook. Or, consider a couple arguing over whether to get an air conditioner. She can't stand the heat but he objects violently because he gets "air-conditioner colds" all the time in the office. Perhaps the air in the office is too dry, or the attic of their house needs an exhaust fan, and so on. A mindful attitude may not avoid all need for compromise, but then again, it might. In any case, it can significantly reduce the margin of conflict. In a domestic setting and, as we will see later, in the workplace or in the realm of prejudice, mindful new distinctions and differentiated categories can smooth the way we get along.

Welcoming New Information

A mindful state also implies openness to new information. Like category making, the receiving of new information is a basic function of living creatures. In fact, lack of new information can be harmful. Research on sensory deprivation shows that, if confined to an unstimulating environment for a long time, such as a submarine or a specially designed, stimulus-free chamber, we suffer a variety of psychological problems. Also, if exposed to patterns of stimulation that are perceived as repeated and unvarying, the sensory system often shuts down, since it is not "receiving" anything new.

A model of mindful receptivity is the inertial navigation system in modern aircraft. This device is constantly receiving new information, constantly letting the pilot know where the plane is at any particular moment. We have a similar mechanism operating within us as we walk or balance ourselves in other ways. Our minds, however, have a tendency to block out small, inconsistent signals.

For example, if a familiar quotation is *altered* so that it is made nonsensical (but retains sufficient structural familiarity), someone reading it out loud is likely to read the *original* quote. Even though what she was reading was not on the page in front of her, she is likely to express great confidence that the the quote was indeed read accurately.[4] (Reread the last sentence, and note the double *the*.) In contrast, mindfully engaged individuals will actively attend to changed signals. Behavior generated from mindful listening or watching, from an expanding, increasingly differentiated information base, is, of course, likely to be more effective.

Consider a relationship between two business partners, Mr. X and Mrs. Y. Perhaps they sense that although the business is growing, misunderstandings are multiplying as well. Mr. X notices that Mrs. Y is categorizing him as rigid. Attuned to subtleties, he feels a lack of approval. Realizing that he and Mrs. Y are very different, but that she may see his style as inappropriate rather than different, he explains his behavior from his own point of view, saying how hard he tries to be consistent and predictable. Mrs. Y accepts Mr. X's depiction of his behavior, now realizing the value of a business partner she can depend upon, instead of seeing these same qualities as rigid. Mrs. Y was able to make this switch because she, too, was open to cues, to another point of view. In the strongest relationships, this sets up a continuous feedback loop that keeps the partnership, marriage, or team in balance, like an aircraft.

More Than One View

Openness, not only to new information, but to different points of view is also an important feature of mindfulness. For years, social psychologists have written about the differences between the perspective of an actor and that of an observer.[5] For instance, we are likely to blame circumstances for our own negative behavior: "The subway always makes me late." If the very same behavior is engaged in by someone else, however, we tend to blame that individual: "He is chronically behind schedule."

Once we become mindfully aware of views other than our own, we start to realize that there are as many different views as there are different observers. Such awareness is potentially liberating. For instance, imagine that someone has just told you that you are rude.

You thought you were being frank. If there is only one perspective, you can't both be right. But with an awareness of many perspectives, you could accept that you are both right and concentrate on whether your remarks had the effect that you actually wanted to produce. If we cling to our own point of view, we may be blind to our impact on others; if we are too vulnerable to other people's definitions of our behavior, we may feel undermined, for observers are typically less flattering of us than we are of ourselves. It is easy to see that any single gesture, remark, or act between people can have *at least* two interpretations: spontaneous versus impulsive; consistent versus rigid; softhearted versus weak; intense versus overemotional; and so on.

This list should not give the impression that for every act there are two set, polarized interpretations. As we said, there are potentially as many interpretations as there are observers. Every idea, person, or object is potentially simultaneously many things depending on the perspective from which it is viewed. A steer is steak to a rancher, a sacred object to a Hindu, and a collection of genes and proteins to a molecular biologist. Nor does being mindful mean that we can plan certain defined ways of interacting with others that will produce certain outcomes; rather, it means that we remain aware that the various possible perspectives will never be exhausted. We can see this on a grand scale or in the most ordinary circumstances. The nuclear accident at Chernobyl was portrayed in many different colors, from a "heroic sacrifice to the benefit of mankind" to "gross and destructive negligence."[6]

Closer to home, we can see how one set of circumstances gives rise to more than one view: "I go regularly to visit my mother—every week, for years now, every week—like clockwork," says a grown-up son. His elderly mother sees things differently: "He's so unpredictable, I never even know what day of the week he's coming. For years now, sometimes it's Monday, sometimes it's not until Friday. I never know."[7]

Or take the couple in Woody Allen's film *Annie Hall*, who were asked by their respective therapists how often they made love. "Hardly ever," says the man, "no more than three times a week." "Constantly," says the woman, "at least three times a week."

As observers, we judge behavior according to whether, as actors, we could or would do the same thing. If I take a basketball shot from the outer key (and make it), I am looked at as though I took a risk. What that means is that my *perceived* competence exceeded someone else's estimates of her own competence. It does not mean that I took more of a risk than someone else would have, had she felt as confident as I. I took the shot because I believed I could make it. However, since the observer would not have risked the shot and does not know my perceived level of competence, she presumes that I'm a *risk taker*. Enjoying the compliment, I do not argue. But being aware of all these elements is in the nature of mindfulness.

In trying to develop a limber state of mind, it helps to remember that people may have perfectly good reasons for behavior we consider negative. Even if their reasons are hard for us, as observers, to discern, people are rarely *intentionally* stingy, grim, choosy, inflexible, secretive, lax, indiscreet, rash, or fussy, for example. No one tries to cultivate unpleasant qualities. Take the same list and imagine yourself in a situation where the word might be applied to you. If you bought someone a present on sale, for instance, would you then see yourself as stingy or thrifty? If you took your children out of school early one Friday in spring, would you see yourself as irresponsible or fun-loving? Virtually all behavior can be cast in a negative or a more tolerable or justifiable light.[8]

The consequences of trying out different perspectives are important. First, we gain more choice in how to respond. A single-minded label produces an automatic reaction, which reduces our options. Also, to understand that other people may not be so different allows us empathy and enlarges our range of responses. We are less likely to feel locked into a polarized struggle.

Second, when we apply this open-minded attitude to our own behavior, change becomes more possible. When I used to do clinical work, it often seemed odd to me that many people in therapy not only had strong motivation to change (hence their visits to me), but the desired behavior was already in their repertoires. What was stopping them? In looking back, now I realize that, often, they were probably trying to change behavior (for example, "being impulsive") that they actively enjoyed, but from another point of view ("being spontaneous"). With this realization, changing one's behavior might be seen not as changing something negative but as making a choice between two positive alternatives (for example, "being reflective" versus "being spontaneous").

One of my students, Loralyn Thompson, and I tested the hypothesis that the reason some people have a hard time changing their behavior, no matter how hard they seem to try, is that they really value that behavior under a different name.[9] Using a list of negative traits, such as rigid, grim, gullible, and the like, we asked people to tell us whether they had tried to change this particular quality about themselves and succeeded or failed, or whether the description was irrelevant to them. Later we had people tell us how much they valued each of a number of traits such as consistency, seriousness, trust, and so on, which were the mirror opposites of the negative traits. Our hypothesis was confirmed. People valued specific qualities that, when negatively framed, were the very things they wanted most to change about themselves but had failed to change. Being aware of these dual views should increase our sense of control and our success in changing behavior (if we still feel that the behavior is undesirable). In Chapter 10 we will see the power of a flexible perspective as it applies to recovery from serious illness and also to therapy for addictions.

Control over Context: The Birdman of Alcatraz

The increased control made possible by mindfulness can also help us change contexts. Irving Janis, John

Wolfer, and I investigated the influence on pain of a single-minded view of the hospital setting.[10] Patients are often certain that pain is inevitable in a hospital. Caught in such a mindset, they assume that, without the help of medication, pain cannot be controlled. In our experiment, we tried to learn whether people could control their experience of pain by putting it in a different, more optimistic context.

Patients who were about to undergo major surgery were taught to imagine themselves in one of two situations: playing football or preparing for a dinner party. In the midst of a rough skirmish on the football field, bruises are hardly noticed. Similarly, cutting oneself while rushing to prepare dinner for ten people who will be arriving any minute might also be something one would hardly notice. In contrast, a paper cut suffered while reading a dull magazine article quickly becomes the focus of attention. Through examples of this sort, participants in the study were taught that, rather than being inevitable, much of the pain we experience appears to be context-dependent.

Hospital staff, unaware of our hypothesis, monitored the use of medication and length of stay for the participating patients in this experimental group and in control groups. Those patients who were taught to reinterpret the hospital experience in nonthreatening ways took fewer pain relievers and sedatives and tended to leave the hospital sooner than the untrained patients. The same hospital experience seen through psychologically different eyes is not the same experience, and the difference could be measured in lower doses of medication and quicker recoveries. This reappraisal technique effectively loosened the hospital mindset and, by showing that pain was not a certainty, gave the participants more control over their convalescence.

Even the most apparently fixed and certain situations can become subject to control if viewed mindfully. The Birdman of Alcatraz was sentenced to life in prison with no hope of reprieve. All the world was cut off from him; one empty, grim day followed the next, as he stared at the flocks of birds flying outside his window. One morning a crippled sparrow happened into his cell, and he nursed it back to health. The bird was no longer just a bird; for him it was a particular sparrow. Other prisoners, guards, visitors started giving him birds and he learned more and more about them. Soon he had a veritable aviary in his cell. He became a distinguished authority on bird diseases, noticing more and more about these creatures and developing more and more expertise. Everything he did was self-taught and original.

Instead of living a dull, stale existence in a cell for forty-odd years, the Birdman of Alcatraz found that boredom can be just another construct of the mind, no more certain than freedom. There is always something new to notice. And he turned what might have been an absolute hell into, at the least, a fascinating, mindful purgatory.

Process Before Outcome

As we saw in Chapter 3, a preoccupation with outcome can make us mindless. Turning this observation around, as we have with all our definitions of mindlessness, we can see mindfulness as a process orientation. Consider a scientist who feels stupid for not having read a journal article that is being discussed heatedly among his colleagues. A mindless hindsight makes him feel this way. He sees himself as having had the choice of either reading or not reading the important article, and having stupidly made the wrong choice. Had he been less fixated on the outcome of the choice, he might have realized that the choice had not been between reading the article and doing nothing, but rather between reading the article or working in the lab, taking a much-needed rest, or reading to his daughter. This is another example of the *faulty comparisons* described in the previous chapter. Awareness of the process of making real choices along the way makes it less likely that we will feel guilty in retrospect. After all, mindful choices are perceived to offer some benefit, or why would we intentionally make them? On occasion, after learning the consequences of a choice, we may wish we had chosen differently, but we still tend not to be quite as hard on ourselves when we know why we did what we did.

A true process orientation also means being aware that every outcome is preceded by a process. Graduate students forget this all the time. They begin their dissertations with inordinate anxiety because they have seen other people's completed and polished work and mistakenly compare it to their own first tentative steps. With their noses deep in file cards and half-baked hypotheses, they look in awe at Dr. So-and-so's published book as if it had been born without effort or false starts, directly from brain to printed page. By investigating how someone got somewhere, we are more likely to see the achievement as hard-won and our own chances as more plausible.

Our judgments about the intelligence of others can be distorted by an emphasis on outcome. In an informal inquiry, my students and I asked people to evaluate the intelligence of scientists who had achieved an "impressive" intellectual outcome (such as discovering a new planet or inventing a new drug). When the achievement was described as a series of steps (and virtually all achievements can be broken down in this way), they judged the scientist as less smart than when the discovery or invention was simply named. People can imagine themselves taking steps, while great heights seem entirely forbidding.

A process orientation not only sharpens our judgment, it makes us feel better about ourselves. A purely outcome orientation can take the joy out of life. Take playing golf. First you learn to keep your head low and not to bend your arm. You keep trying and you lower your score. But imagine that you read about clubs that would decrease your score by a third. Wouldn't you buy them? The fourth hole in four rather than six strokes—that's playing. Now to get better golf balls. Ah, down to three strokes. Finally a new ball is invented, so refined that it finds its way to the hole on one stroke. What a game, a hole in one on each stroke. What game?

In a game, we can understand that process—if not being everything—is really all that matters. But it may be the same for the rest of our lives. In business, would it be nice always to be assured of success? What if every business plan worked out, without stumbling blocks or irritations? At first it might seem appealing, like the Midas touch. What would such a life be like? A corporate nursing home? According to the Japanese, big business has a lot to learn from kindergarten children. In some Japanese firms, the thinkers and innovators are specifically encouraged to be *process-oriented*—the results can come later.[11] Bell Labs, with its focus on research, was said to be free from a drive toward products, at least until the breakup of AT&T.

Mindfulness East and West

The definitions of mindfulness in this chapter, especially the process orientation just discussed, will remind many readers of various concepts of mindfulness found in Eastern religion. Students in my classes who are knowledgeable about such fields are continually drawing parallels. While there are many similarities, the differences in the historical and cultural background from which they are derived, and the more elaborate methods, including meditation, through which a mindful state is said to be achieved in the Eastern traditions should make us cautious about drawing comparisons that are too tidy.

My work on mindfulness has been conducted almost entirely within the Western scientific perspective. Initially, my focus was on mindlessness and its prevalence in daily life. As can be seen in the order of chapters so far in this book, the notion of mindfulness develops gradually by looking at aspects of mindlessness and then at the other side of the coin. Only after a series of experiments demonstrating the costs of rigid mindsets and single-minded perspectives do I begin to explore the enormous potential benefits of a mindful attitude in aging, health, creativity, and the workplace.

Behind Eastern teachings of mindfulness lies an elaborate system of cosmology developed and refined over time. The moral aspect of mindfulness (the idea that the mindful state achieved through meditation will lead to spontaneous right action[12]) is an essential part of these philosophies. It reaches into matters too complex for the scope of this book. Since many qualities of the Eastern concepts of mindfulness and of the one being described in this book are strikingly similar, however, we might hope that some of the moral consequences striven for by the Eastern disciplines might also result from mindfulness as understood in this Western form and context.

As an example of the semantic and philosophical tangles that arise if we try to compare Eastern and Western views of the mindful state, consider the activity of creating new categories. While this is a form of mindfulness in our definition, it appears to be in direct opposition to what one does during meditation.[13] In meditation, the mind becomes quieter and active thought is discouraged. In some forms of meditation, thoughts and images that come to mind are considered unimportant and are relinquished as soon as one discerns their presence. At the same time, in many Eastern views, the proper meditation techniques are said to result in a state that has been called *de-automatization*.[14] In this state, old categories break down and the individual is no longer trapped by stereotypes. Such freedom from rigid distinctions is very similar to the mindfulness being described in this book. This one example should show why, not being fully trained in Eastern thought, I leave it to others to tease out the similarities and differences between the two concepts of mindfulness. If a reader is familiar with a particular Eastern discipline, she or he may enjoy making comparisons, in both technique and result.

CHAPTER 6

*

Mindful Aging

When a new disability arrives I look about to see if death has come, and I call quietly, "Death, is that you? Are you there?" So far the disability has answered, "Don't be silly, it's me."
FLORIDA SCOTT-MAXWELL, *The Measure of My Days*

*

Age is such a potent marker that whatever happens to our minds and bodies in later life, we assume it to be the result of advancing years. If older people do anything the least bit unusual, we label it eccentricity or senility, even if they have been doing the same thing all their lives. Within such constricting mindsets, tight as an undersized suit of armor, growth, flexibility, and new enterprise become impossible. Not only the quality but the length of our lives may be affected.

Control and Survival

The costs of mindlessness, and the potential benefits of increasing mindfulness, became particularly clear to me while conducting research with the elderly. In 1976, with Judith Rodin, a colleague from Yale, I explored the effects of decision making and responsibility on residents in a nursing home.[1] We divided the residents into an experimental and a control group. Those in the experimental group were emphatically encouraged to make more decisions for themselves. We tried to come up with decisions that mattered and at the same time would not disturb the staff. For example, these residents were asked to choose where to receive visitors: inside the home or outdoors, in their rooms, in the dining room, in the lounge, and so on. They were also told that a movie would be shown the next week on Thursday and Friday and that they should decide whether they wanted to see it and, if so, when. In addition to choices of this sort, residents in the experimental group were each given a houseplant to care for. They were to choose when and how much to water the plants, whether to put them in the window or to shield them from too much sun, and so forth.

This group was contrasted with members of a comparison group who were also given plants but were told that the nurses would take care of them. Those in the comparison group were not encouraged to make decisions for themselves but were told that the staff was there to help them in every way possible. For example, if they wanted to visit with people inside the home or outside the home, in their room, in the dining room, or in the lounge, we suggested that they tell a member of the staff, who would help them arrange it. We tried to make the issues between the two groups as similar as possible except for the distinctions about who was responsible and in control.

Before the experiment began and three weeks after it ended, we used various behavioral and emotional measures to judge the effect of this encouragement. Measures of behavior (like participation in activities of the nursing home), subjective reports (how happy residents felt), and ratings by the staff (how alert and active they judged the residents to be) all showed clear and dramatic improvement for the group that had been given more responsibility.

Eighteen months after the study, we went back to the nursing home and took the same measures. The residents who had been given more responsibility still took more initiative, and were significantly more active, vigorous, and sociable than the others. When Judith Rodin gave a lecture at the nursing home, she found that those who participated actively and asked the most questions came from the experimental group. At that time we also measured the residents' physical health. While, before our study began, the health evaluation ratings of the two groups (based on their medical records) had been the same, eighteen months later the health of the experimental group had improved while that of the comparison group had worsened. The most striking discovery, however, was that the changed attitudes we had initiated in these nursing home residents resulted in a lower mortality rate. Only seven of the forty-seven subjects in the experimental group had died during the eighteen-month period, whereas thirteen of the forty-four subjects in the comparison group had died (15 percent versus 30 percent).

Because these results were so startling, we looked for other factors that might have affected the death rates. Unfortunately, we cannot have known everything about the residents prior to our experiment. We do know that those who died did not differ significantly in the length of time that they had been in the institution or, as pointed out, in their overall health status when the study began. The actual causes of death that appeared on the medical records varied from one individual to another in both groups. Thus, the larger number of deaths in the comparison group was not the result of a certain disease being more prevalent in one group than in another. The changes brought about by the experiment in the lives of the residents did seem to lead, literally and figuratively, to more living. When we look closely at our "treatment"—encouraging choice and decision making and giving residents something *new* to look after—it seems appropriate to see it as a way of increasing mindfulness. These results have been confirmed by much research since that time.

Among other effects, increased mindfulness appears to reduce the depression associated with old age. Larry Perlmuter and I looked at whether we could decrease depression as well as increase self-knowledge and memory through a behavioral monitoring technique.[2] This technique, in which subjects take note of the choices they make in daily activities, had already been shown to be an effective way to increase mindfulness.[3] It rests on an assumption about the nature of choice: The opportunity to make choices increases our motivation. In most of our ordinary activities, however, the potential choices that once existed are long forgotten. If I have orange juice for breakfast every day, even though there are many alternatives available, chances are I am not making a meaningful choice. Meaningful choice involves some awareness of the other alternatives that have not been selected. Through this awareness we learn something about ourselves, our tastes and preferences. For instance, if I stop to ask myself why I'm not having grapefruit or tomato juice, I would know it was not just that I wanted something cold, since all of them are cold; and not that I wanted a citrus flavor, since both grapefruit and orange offer that. Perhaps I wanted something sweet and citrusy. Distinctions like this, in such minor but also in more important ways, make us aware of how we are shaping our days.

Both retirees and residents of nursing homes participated in this pilot study. They were introduced to one of four ways to monitor their daily choices over an extended period of time. The types of monitoring varied in the complexity of the thinking required, and also in the amount of control exercised by the subjects. We assumed that more complicated thinking and more control would increase mindfulness.

The first ("least mindful") group was asked simply to monitor and evaluate particular activities each day for a week (for example, the first drink they chose during the day). The second group monitored different behaviors each day. The third group was asked to focus on different activities each day, but also to list, for each one, three alternatives they could have selected but did not. The last ("most mindful") group was the same as the third group, except the subjects chose which activities to monitor. At the conclusion of the week-long experiment, the subjects were interviewed and rated by independent observers as to mood, degree of independence and confidence, and alertness.

For virtually each measure, the more decisions and control required of the subjects, the more likely they were to have become (1) less depressed; (2) more independent and confident; and (3) more alert and differentiated in their choices. These initial results make a strong case for further research into this aspect of aging. We would not expect the findings to hold if so many decisions are thrust on someone at once that, instead of making one at a time, the person might choose not to make any.

Surprisingly, we found a lot of unintentional resistance—from families and the elderly themselves—to our attempts to give them more control and make them more independent. As in many institutional settings, dependency is unwittingly but flagrantly encouraged.[4] When a nursing home resident is helped to dress for breakfast (either out of concern for the resident or to save time for the staff), he or she may feel incompetent and helpless. Ultimately such help will take more of the staff's time, since the more help people are given, the more help they will come to need.[5] Once, arriving at a nursing home before the visit scheduled for a research project, I fell into a discussion with an eighty-year-old woman who had come to visit her eighty-four-year-old sister. She told me that her sister asked her to bring her some wooden tongs so that she could put on her underwear without help, for it was hard for her to bend over. I asked her if she bought them for her sister, and she said firmly, "Heavens no; if she used them she'd probably hurt her back." Appalled at her reply I suggested jokingly that perhaps we should consider inducing a semi-comatose state. That way we could be sure she wouldn't fall and break her hip, or choke. She chuckled and quickly saw the point. Well-meant protectiveness gradually undermines any autonomy. And more coercive interference, such as tying residents into their chairs all day to keep them from "hurting themselves," defeats any shred of initiative.

Watching someone else do things that we used to do ourselves leads us to feel that we are now incapable of doing them. This is true even when the only reason for our inaction is outside ourselves (institutional policy, for example). Mindsets about old age confirm a sense of incompetence. It is unlikely that an old person will find a flattering explanation for why she isn't doing something for herself. When there is one ready explanation for something—being old—we rarely search for other possible causes. Since no one bothers to find out just what the old person can or can't do, a lowest-common-denominator level of care is administered. When the will to act is thwarted, it atrophies into a wish to be taken care of.

Reversing Memory Loss

Perhaps the most common problem blamed on aging is loss of memory. I remember waking up one summer morning and not being able to remember what day it was. Had I been eighty, I would not have looked far for the reason. Since I was less than half that age, I puzzled over this lapse and realized that in July, with no classes to teach and no appointments to keep, every day was pretty much the same as every other. There was no reason to remember whether it was Tuesday or Wednesday, so I didn't.

The experience gave me an increased interest in the memory loss associated with age. Were there reasons for it instead of or in addition to advancing years, and was it reversible? With several colleagues, I designed some experiments to see whether giving people more reason to remember made memory loss reversible.[6] In one of these studies, residents of a nursing home were visited nine times over a three-week period. We set up one experimental and two control groups. During each visit we made increasingly difficult cognitive demands, including questions of various levels of difficulty concerning the nursing home. For instance, we asked, "How many nurses' and patients' names do you know?"; and "When will the next cocktail party (or bingo game, or concert) take place?" If the resident did not know, he or she was asked to find out by the next visit. Other questions concerned meals and daily activities. For each correct answer residents were given chips which were redeemable for a gift. One control group was questioned in the same way but given the chips only as mementos and not for motivation. A second comparison group was not given either the various challenges or the chips.

All the groups were given tests of short-term memory, as well as nurses' ratings for alertness, at the beginning and the end of the experiment. The experimental group outperformed both of the other groups on these measures. We also looked at medical records and found that at the end of the study, overall health was better for the experimental group than for the comparison group. A follow-up study[7] two-and-a-half years later showed that the benefits of this type of mindfulness training also included an effect on survival. Only 7 percent of the experimental group had died, compared with 33 percent and 27 percent of the two comparison groups. Since several other residents in the comparison groups, but only one in the experimental group, had left to go to the hospital, where many of them subsequently died, the difference in long-term benefits between the experimental group and the comparison groups is probably even greater.

Outgrowing Mindsets

Many of the options and choices and opportunities to be responsible that we provide in our experiments are part of an old person's daily life in other cultures. For instance, here is how the older members of the Yadhan (a tribe now vanished) were regarded:

Their opinion is valued. If they are intelligent and upright they have great influence. Some aged widows are the heads of families, and they are strictly obeyed. The old people's experience is useful to the community: they know how to find food and carry out the household tasks. It is they who hand on the unwritten law and cause it to be respected. They give a good example, and if the occasion arises they correct and even punish those who behave badly.[8]

Despite the fact that many of us know very few elderly adults personally, we have very strong ideas about aging. Many of these ideas are premature cognitive commitments. As we saw in the study discussed at the end of Chapter 3, positive mindsets about old age may result in richer aging. Those who had been exposed to a more optimistic image of old age in their youth were more alert and more active in old age. But this is not the image most of us carry. When we are young, we hear expressions like "old bat," "doddering old fool," "poor little old lady" from people with very negative views of old age before we ever start thinking of ourselves as potentially old people.

The longer we are alive, the more opportunity there is for something that was once irrelevant, and to which we have already made a premature cognitive commitment, to become relevant.

Consider our attitudes toward nursing homes. In Cambridge, Massachusetts, I met an eighty-three-year-old woman named Mildred who has been in a nursing home for two years. The food is good, and so is the care. But Mildred had lived for many years in an old Cambridge house among neighbors who had grown old along with her and among trees older than them all. She loved her house. But Mildred got older, less able to take care of herself, and the money ran out. The house was sold and Mildred moved to the nursing home. A former teacher, she loves paperback books, though today she reads very little. They are now her sole companions, lying scattered about like stuffed animals. When I visited her I asked her about Harry Truman, who was a pupil of hers when she taught writing in Washington, D.C.: "I used to go walking with President Truman, when he was president. He was a nice man." Apparently Truman wanted to improve his English and Mildred helped him.

When I asked more about Truman, Mildred wanted to change the subject. "You hear all these reasons why people come to a place like this," she said. "Well, they're here because they have no place left to go."

Mildred's view of nursing homes reflects an accurate but unnecessary fact. Because most people share this view, nursing homes match these negative images. Not only is it painful to hold this negative view if a nursing home turns out to be our new home, which it very well might, but such negative views in younger people help create the reality of nursing homes as grim dead ends. Such is the power of mindsets.

Much of what older people experience could be the result of negative stereotypes, internalized in childhood. We do not know how many of the "infirmities of age" are actually genetically programmed into our bodies, or how many may be due to premature cognitive commitments. We do not know how many more serene or exciting options for living one's later life might be conjured up if our minds were open to them.

Cicero said, "So feeble are many old men that they cannot execute any task or duty or any function of life whatever, but that in Truth is not the peculiar fault of old age, but belongs to bad health."[9] Old age and poor health continue to be confused.[10] Illness may be more likely in old age, but it is not the same thing as old age. By unquestioningly assuming that old age means frailty and weakness, we expect little of the old people around us, and of ourselves as we grow older. The consequence of such mindsets is an interactive spiral gradually wearing us down. Self-esteem, of course, is undermined and causes more suffering because elderly people blame themselves rather than the situations they are in. An experiment is described at the end of this chapter that may give readers ideas about how to circumvent the worn mindsets and surprise themselves with a renewed old age. In it we essentially tricked the body to step back twenty years.

Florida Scott-Maxwell, a Jungian analyst who did

not begin her training until midlife, began writing a private notebook at the age of eighty-two, in which she recorded her impressions of old age. Her experiences, mindfully observed, did not fit her expectations: "Age puzzles me. I thought it was a quiet time. My seventies were interesting and fairly serene, but my eighties are passionate. . . . To my own surprise I burst out with hot conviction."[11]

Stretching the Limits of Age

What exactly are our mindsets about old age? Ann Mulvey and I ran a study to find out what actions are most commonly cited as characteristic of older people.[12] The study implicitly asked: Is being old seen as akin to being senile? We used questionnaires to evaluate beliefs about the behavior of older people, and to determine whether information and attitudes about senile behavior vary as a function of age and/or familiarity with the elderly. Our subjects were 75 adults: 25 between the ages of 25 and 40; 25 between the ages of 45 and 60; and 25 over the age of 70.

We asked subjects to list those kinds of behavior that they thought were characteristic of people in three different age groups: 25–35, 65–75, and 76 or older. We also asked them which of these kinds of behavior, if any, indicated senility. Next, all participants read the same descriptions of various events and were asked to describe what a senile person would be likely to do in each situation. For example, "A senile person walks into

a store and picks up a loaf of bread. He or she then
_____." Finally, respondents were asked how likely it
was that they themselves would become senile.

Judges who were unaware of the experimental hypotheses rated the replies. The young and middle-aged
subjects saw old people as involved primarily in non-
social behavior and passive activities, and as possessing
unpleasant personal characteristics to a much greater
extent than positive ones. The elderly subjects, on the
other hand, viewed older people as significantly more
involved in social activities and possessing more appealing personal qualities. The younger population was
more likely than the old to view the elderly as sickly.

For old, middle-aged, and young subjects alike,
there appeared to be a stereotype of the elderly adult
that included a fairly well-defined idea of senility. Each
age group viewed senility in very negative terms and
called it a condition of physical deterioration causing
memory loss, mental incompetence, loss of contact with
reality, and helplessness. In addition, and most interestingly, we found that over 65 percent of the younger
group felt certain that *they* would *not* become senile,
while only 10 percent of the elderly group expressed
this certainty. To turn this around, a full *90 percent* of
the elderly subjects felt that there was a good chance
they would become senile, even though, according to
medical accounts, only 4 percent of those over 64 suffer
from a severe form of senility, and only another 10
percent suffer from a milder version.[13]

When we are young and answer questions about
old age, we do so with the feeling that we will never

grow old. In the meantime, we form mindsets about the relationship between debilitated performance and old age. Once we awaken to an old self, those relationships become threatening and the fears begin. Such fears are inhibiting and likely to discourage older people from trying to extend themselves in new ways.

Growth in Age

The notion that the aging process and the physiological deterioration that accompanies it are the inevitable results of the passage of time sets us up for a self-fulfilling prophecy. It is hard to challenge. As we saw in Chapter 2, time in our culture is essentially regarded as a linear phenomenon. While many modern philosophers, as we saw, have rejected the linear model of time in favor of a variety of other concepts, it is still that model that constrains our view of human development. Within this view, most of us see aging as a process in which the body (and, consequently, the person) is inevitably worn down, after reaching peak efficiency in the earlier stages of life. Such a process, however, does not apply at the level of elementary particles or units of energy. On a macroscopic level there appears to be gradual dissolution from organization to disorganization, a "growing older" if you will, at least in a closed system. But when we look at the atoms that make up a person (old or young), a tree, or a pillow, they stay the same over time. The behavioral and social sciences, however, are still largely entrenched in a linear conception of time and an associated image of universal entropy.

Cognitive skills and psychological and physical health are presumed to be curvilinearly related to age. In this view, the individual grows to maturity and then lives out the adult years of life adjusting to diminishing capacities. Some cultures incorporate the growth of wisdom into their accounts of human aging. However, this continuing growth of wisdom is usually seen as a stream of development that is either independent of, or occurs in reaction to, a process of decline that is taking place in other areas.

In one possible alternative view of the life cycle, the path that we traverse from birth to death is a series of goal-directed mini-trajectories, relatively independent of one another. In this view, the past has less overall influence on behavior. Within any one of these separate trajectories, the mind may be more powerful in shaping development.

It is interesting to note how rarely the term *development* is used to describe changes in the later years. Despite current emphasis on a lifespan perspective, change in later years is still typically described as *aging*. In the same way, although the word *day* can refer to the twenty-four-hour span, we normally use it to refer to only the brighter hours. *Aging* has come to refer to the darker side of growing older. To make changes in later life one must fight against all sorts of popular mindsets.

When we are behaving mindlessly, that is to say,

relying on categories drawn in the past, endpoints to development seem fixed. We are then like projectiles moving along a predetermined course. When we are mindful, we see all sorts of choices and generate new endpoints. Mindful involvement in each episode of development makes us freer to map our own course.

Newly elected President Franklin D. Roosevelt came to call on Justice Oliver Wendell Holmes and asked the older man why he was learning Greek (at his age). "To improve my mind, young man," said Justice Holmes.

One of the few pieces of information about brain physiology that has caught the attention of many lay people is the loss of neurons after a certain age. Any bit of forgetfulness after age thirty is apt to be blamed on this loss. But even this scientific "fact" may not be absolute. Fernando Nottebohm studied the rebirth of neurons in the brains of canaries.[14] Knowing that only male canaries sing, he and his colleagues injected females with testosterone. They too started to sing. Nottebohm reasoned that in the presence of testosterone, new neurons would form when the birds learned songs. He and Steven Goldberg then injected the female birds with either testosterone or a neutral control treatment. They also injected them with a radioactive labeling material which is incorporated into the DNA of dividing cells. For thirty days they repeated the process. To their surprise, the researchers found a massive increase in the number of neurons in both sets of birds, even the females given the control treatment, who did not sing.

In fact, they found this rebirth of neurons occurs in adult birds annually, although testosterone and the learning of new songs were not the relevant factors.

Other research with animals demonstrates the possibility of brain development in adulthood. First, many researchers have found that the brains of animals vary as a result of rearing; those animals reared in complex environments have more dendritic material than animals in control groups.[15] (A *dendrite* is the part of a nerve cell that sends impulses to the cell body.) More exciting is the discovery that environmental complexity introduced in *adulthood* can alter the thickness of the cortex.[16] Brain physiology, chemistry, and anatomy are far more plastic than previously assumed. Despite the assumption that growing old is an irreversible process of physiological decline, some kinds of mental functioning can bring about new growth in tissues.

Most of the arbitrary limits we set on our development in later life are not based on scientific information at all. Our own mental picture of age, based on hundreds of small premature cognitive commitments, will shape the life we lead in our own late adulthood. Before examining specific strategies for changing these images, we might take a look at two more positive images of old age from an earlier century.

Lytton Strachey describes Queen Victoria in her late sixties:

Next year was the fiftieth of her reign and in June the splendid anniversary was celebrated in solemn pomp. Victoria surrounded by the highest dignitaries of her realm, escorted by a glittering galaxy of kings, and princes, drove through the crowded enthusiasm of the capital to render thanks to God in Westminster Abbey. . . . The Queen was hailed at once as the mother of her people and as the embodied symbol of their imperial greatness; and she responded to the double sentiment with all the ardour of her spirit. England and the people of England, she knew it, she felt it, were, in some wonderful and yet quite simple manner, *hers*. Exultation, affection, gratitude, a profound sense of obligation, an unbounded pride—such were her emotions; and colouring and intensifying the rest, there was something else. At last, after so long, happiness —fragmentary, perhaps, and charged with gravity, but true and unmistakable none the less—had returned to her.[17]

The feelings Strachey describes are not restricted to those who rule the British empire. A visit from one's grandchildren could evoke similar emotions.

William James's letter to his dying father conveys the same respectful, admiring view of age—an enormous contrast to the mindsets described earlier.

Meanwhile, my blessed old Father, I scribble this line (which may reach you though I should come too late), just to tell you how full of the tenderest memories and feelings about you my heart has for the last few days been filled. In that mysterious gulf of the past into which the present soon will fall and go back and back, yours is still for me the central figure. All my intellectual life I derive from you; and though we have often seemed at odds in the expression thereof, I'm sure there's a harmony somewhere, and that our strivings will combine. What my debt to you is goes beyond all my power of estimating—so early, so penetrating and so constant has been the influence. You need be in no anxiety about your literary remains. I will see them well taken care of, and that your words shall not suffer for being concealed. . . .

As for us, we shall live on in this way—feeling somewhat unprotected, old as we are for the absence of the parental bosoms as a refuge, but holding fast together in that common sacred memory. We will stand by each other and by Alice, try to transmit the torch in our offspring as you did in us, and when the time comes for being gathered in, I pray we may, if not all, some at least, be as ripe as you.[18]

We cannot be sure why some people age mindfully, nor can we know whether admiring views of older people stem from positive mindsets about aging or from mindfulness. What we do know is that models like these help all of us age a little better.

Putting Age in Context: An Experiment

If negative premature cognitive commitments lead to unhealthy images of aging, can we reverse premature cognitive commitments and improve health? Together with a group of graduate students at Harvard, I designed a study to investigate this question.[19] We attempted to invoke in a group of elderly subjects a state of mind that they had experienced twenty years ago, and to see whether their bodies also "backtracked" to a more youthful state. The attempt could be seen as an experiment in context control. We enlisted the help of a group of elderly men who agreed to try to place themselves in a time-altered context and allow us to take physical as well as psychological measurements. These men's bodies were seventy-five to eighty years old, and we were going to encourage the state of mind they had at fifty-five. We knew this had not been done before, and *any* positive results would be meaningful since old age is taken to be a one-way street to incapacitation. Demonstrable physiological changes would confirm that psychological factors contribute to the way humans age and develop. They would also provide more evidence that the aging process is less fixed than most people think.

We tested our hypothesis by comparing the effects of two experiences: in one, participants made a psychological attempt to *be* the person they were twenty years ago; and in the other, participants merely focused on that past of twenty years ago. We designed the study so that as far as content was concerned, the two groups would be occupied with essentially similar thoughts. The major difference between the two groups that could account for any difference in results would be the context in which the two experiences took place.

The context for the experimental group was the way things were twenty years ago, while for the control group the context was the present. The challenge was to get the experimental group "into context" and then get them to go about their usual routine.

We placed an advertisement in a newspaper calling for male subjects over seventy years old. Those in reasonably good health were selected as our research participants. We arranged to take them to a country retreat for five days, where they were encouraged through props and instructions either to step back into the past or to view the past from the present. Accordingly, for the former group all conversation about the past was to be held in the *present* tense, while for the latter conversation about the past was in the *past* tense.

Several sets of measurements were made before the experimental week actually began and again on Day 5. Some were repeated throughout the week. They measured physical strength, perception, cognition, taste, hearing, and visual thresholds. The particular measures used reflected the "biological markers" recommended by geriatricians. (Interestingly, these leading physicians said there were no clear markers.[20]) Measurements included the following: hand grip, bideltoid breadth, triceps skinfold, finger length, weight, height, gait, and posture. We measured vision with and without eyeglasses, and administered a series of paper-and-pencil maze tests that would assess speed of completion and accuracy. In a test of visual memory, the participants were asked to look at a figure drawing for ten seconds and then wait ten seconds before reproducing the figure from memory with paper and pencil. Finally, each subject was also asked to fill out a self-rating form called SYMLOG that assesses values and behavior[21].

Participants chosen for the experiment had been sent an information packet in the mail containing a program for the week that mentioned testing, meals, discussions, each evening's activities, general instructions, a floor plan of the retreat including the location of their rooms, and a request for subjects not to bring any magazines, newspapers, books, or family pictures more recent than 1959. We had also previously asked for photographs of the participants from the recent past and from twenty years ago. The group that was to step into the past received the photographs of each of their fellow group members as they appeared approximately twenty years earlier, while the comparison group was given recent photographs. Information in the packet also included detailed suggestions about what clothes to bring.

On the first day of orientation the participants wrote an autobiographical sketch. The instructions read: "Specifically, the autobiography should describe you (your likes, dislikes, activities, jobs, relationships, joys, worries, etc.) as you were about 20 years ago. In fact, please focus on 1959. Please note that it is important that you be accurate. Then, begin with the day you were born and work up to the present." These directions were the same for both groups. However, the experimental group was further asked to: "Write (and talk) in the *present tense* about the past. Remember that the 'present' means 1959. So do not include any of your history past this date." We stressed the importance of this instruction before the experiment began, since speaking in the present tense about the past was to be our primary strategy.

Participants arrived at Harvard University early on the first morning. After being introduced to one another, they were asked to attend a short orientation meeting. We told the participants that one purpose of our study of reminiscence was to gather information about people in their late fifties, and we said that we believed one way to obtain new material about this age group was to question older people about their experience at that earlier time in their lives. They were told that to encourage memory of their personal histories, we wanted to bring similar people together.

While medical measurements were being made for some subjects, others were photographed. Participants, individually and at various times, were asked to go into a different room to pick up another questionnaire. Their gait and posture were videotaped as they entered the room.

After this pretesting, the men were grouped together for our final orientation comments before leaving for the retreat. The control group was told once again that they were to concentrate on the past. We asked them to help each other do this. We told them that we had reason to believe that the discussions we had planned for them, coupled with the other activities, which would all take place in a very beautiful environment, might have very positive effects on them. They might improve their physical health as well as their psychological well-being. "In fact," we said, "you may feel as well as you did in 1959."

In contrast, the orientation remarks for the experimental group stressed that the best way to learn about the past may not be through simple reminiscence. Rather, we should try to return as completely as possible in our minds to that earlier time. "Therefore, we're going together to a very beautiful retreat where we will live as if it were 1959. Obviously, that means no one can discuss anything that happened after September

1959. It is your job to help each other do this. It is a difficult task since we are not asking you to 'act as if it is 1959' but to let yourself *be* just who you were in 1959. We have good reason to believe that if you are successful at this you will feel as well as you did in 1959." They were told that *all* of their activities and conversations should reflect the "fact" that it is 1959. "It may be difficult at first but the sooner you let yourself go, the more fun you'll have." This group was also led to expect positive effects from the retreat.

All participants were also asked to use the photos they were sent in order to help them come to know each other. Thus, men in the experimental group looked for the twenty-years-younger man in each other. Then the men in the experimental group boarded the van for the retreat. As they departed we reminded them that once they left for the retreat, it would be 1959. In this spirit, a tape of music that was popular in that year, along with commercials advertising products of that time, was played on the van's "radio."

The following week the control group left for the retreat in the van and listened to the current radio programs.

The retreat center is located on approximately ten acres of tree-covered rolling hills set off from the main road— a world in and of itself. Because the men were from different ethnic backgrounds, the religious objects in the retreat buildings were all removed, and what re- mained was a timeless backdrop for our study. We had brought many props for the experimental group, including magazines like *Life* and *The Saturday Evening Post* for the same week in 1959, and we put them in each man's room. For the comparison group there were also old magazines available, but these were from various past years, not just that particular week in 1959.

The program consisted partly of twice-daily structured discussions, followed by lunch and then another discussion. Dinner and free time in the evening were followed by a planned activity. The discussions were about well-defined topics, led by moderators prepared in advance. Each discussion began with a three-minute audiotape about the past played through an old radio (for the experimental group) or a new radio (for the control group). Subjects had been given the questions to be discussed the night before. After the radio broadcast the moderator would engage subjects in discussion for forty-five minutes. For the experimental group discussions were held in the present tense, while the comparison group was free to discuss the issues in the past tense. Each topic had been woven into the activity the night before, which helped provide a context for remembering.

A good 1959 movie was shown the first evening, *Anatomy of a Murder*. ·Right after the movie, participants were given copies of the questions to be discussed the next day. The form said: "Two of the movies which were in the running for the Oscars for 1958 were *Auntie Mame* and *Cat on a Hot Tin Roof.* Which was better and why?"

The men were questioned about the movies. Then the second discussion of the day began; it had to do with sports: "From these following names, who do you think is the best player? Why? Bill Russell, Johnny Unitas, Mickey Mantle, Wilt Chamberlain, Floyd Patterson, Ted Williams, Frank Gifford, Bob Cousy, Warren Spahn, Maurice Richard."

One night the men had a game night and played a version of the old game show "The Price Is Right." We wanted to see whether they would give 1959 prices or current prices for items presented. The following day they had a conversation about financial matters. In the afternoon they heard a speech by President Eisenhower and then discussed politics. That night they were entertained by live musicians, followed the next morning by a discussion about music. Finally, that afternoon they talked about television situation comedies of the past, like "I Love Lucy," "The Honeymooners," and "Sergeant Bilko."

Late in the afternoon of the fourth day of their stay and on the last morning, all of the physical and psychological measures were taken again. A reaction time test was added, measuring the speed of recall of people who were well known in 1959. We asked the participants to look at a presentation of ten slides, one after another, each of which showed one noteworthy figure: Thomas Dewey, Phil Silvers, Jackie Gleason, Groucho Marx, Elvis Presley, Nikita Khrushchev, Milton Berle, Ethel Merman, Fidel Castro, and Douglas MacArthur. For each slide, participants were instructed to press a reaction time key as soon as they recalled the person in the slide. If, after ten seconds, the participant did not remember the person in the slide, he was given a score of ten seconds and told to prepare for the next slide. Once they pressed the key, participants were asked to identify the person. We correctly predicted that the experimental group would perform more quickly and accurately than the control group, since for the former these people seemed like more recent figures.

Also on the last day the men's gaits and postures were videotaped for comparison with the earlier tapes. Discussions were videotaped to see how active participation and ease of conversing in the present tense about the past had changed during the week. Meals were videotaped to document how much and how vigorously the men ate and also whether they took what they needed from the kitchen without waiting to be served, whether they cleaned up after themselves, and so on.

Our results fell into two classes. First, there were measures on which both the experimental and control groups showed significant improvement at the end of the experiment when compared to their at-home baseline level of performance prior to this experiment. These before/after differences are worth noting since they contrast with the psychological and physical *decrements* we usually associate with aging. The change of context in this study seems to have yielded general improvement on these measures.

The men as a whole looked younger by about three years after the experiment. Independent judges evaluated facial photographs at the beginning and end of the study. Even though lighting and printing were held constant, the participants looked younger at the end of the week. There was also a uniform tendency for hearing to improve. Improvement in psychological functioning was made evident in both groups by their steadily more efficient performance on the memory task over the course of the experiment.

The men in both groups ate heartily and, for better or worse, gained an average of three pounds over the week. Bideltoid and tricep skinfolds increased (although here we expected a decrease since people are generally less flabby when they are younger). And, finally, hand strength increased steadily over the week for both groups. By the second day the men were actively involved in serving their meals and cleaning up after they finished. This was quite a change from their evident dependence on the relatives who initially brought them to the study. They were all functioning independently almost as soon as they arrived at the retreat.

Many of these changes might take place if elderly men were simply taken on a vacation. We were not able to find a comparable "vacationing" comparison group, nor could we at the time afford to bring other groups to the retreat to find out whether various other factors might account for our results. We cannot be sure just to what to attribute these changes. Participants in both groups ate well and slept well, probably better than they were used to at home. They were treated with more respect and given more responsibility than is typical for the elderly. In fact, right from the start they were thrust into a situation unlike anything they had recently experienced. When the comparison group first arrived at the retreat, it happened that the doctoral and postdoctoral students who were helping with the experiment were off somewhere picking up equipment, so that no one was there to help with the participants' bags. I looked at all the suitcases. I looked at the participants and then back at the suitcases. Overwhelmed by the thought of carrying them myself, I told the men that they could move them toward their rooms a little at a time, or unpack them where they were and carry the items to their rooms piecemeal if necessary. Whatever they decided, they were responsible for handling their own baggage. This was a big change from the coddling and overhelping to which they had become accustomed.

Perhaps most important, these elderly men were encouraged to take a good deal of control over their lives. Other research that we have already discussed suggests that this variable is indeed powerful.[22] Making demands on the elderly, as we did here, may well have been a big factor in reversing many debilities of old age for both groups of participants.

Differences between the two groups in this study ranged from the striking to the suggestive. Our measure of joint flexibility and finger length increased to a significantly greater degree for the experimental group than for the control group. In fact, finger length increased for over a third of the experimental group and remained the same for the rest of the group, while a third of the comparison group actually worsened on this measure. There was also a greater increase in sitting height for the experimental group than for the control group. They also had gained more weight and had greater increases in tricep skinfold and bideltoid breadth. Performance on the mazes, our measure of manual dexterity, also showed a difference in the two groups. Experimental subjects showed greater manual dexterity. Their errors decreased while the average number of errors for the comparison group increased. In testing vision without glasses on, vision in the right eye improved for the experimental group and slightly worsened for the comparison group.

In addition to these physical changes, we found improvements on psychological tests. The most important of these differences occurred on the intelligence tests we administered (digit symbol, substitution test). Again, the experimental group as a whole improved while the control group's performance worsened somewhat over time. Well over half of the experimental group improved while the performance of a quarter of the control subjects declined.

All was not for the better in the experimental group, however. While the control group changed toward greater friendliness and emotional expressiveness, the experimental group rated themselves as increasingly unfriendly. (This may reflect the fact that they had to work somewhat harder to maintain the time orientation than the comparison group.)

Taken together, these results are impressive, given the way almost all of us look at aging. Change of all kinds, most of it positive, was found in these men at an age when growth and development are considered arrested or in decline.

Recently, as I thought more about these results, I

realized that the very design of the study might reflect an age bias. Why did we think that a seventy-five-year-old would like to be in his fifties again? A forty-year-old cherishes his experience and matured consciousness. We can accept that he might not voluntarily give up his current identity to return to the person he was at twenty. In the same way, the seventy-five-year-old may not be willing to return completely to the world of the fifty-year-old, even though some of the health and strength of the earlier time might be desirable.

The design of our study, however, was motivated not only by the hypothesis that the state of a person's body could be "turned back," if we could shift that person's mind back to where it was twenty years ago, but by an alternative hypothesis. This hypothesis assumed that it took a certain measure of mindfulness for men in both groups to participate in this novel experience, but that a greater degree of mindfulness was required of the experimental group since it had to comply with a set of instructions that were more elaborate than those given to the control group.

If it was this greater mindful activity that occasioned our results, then in principle, *any* intense mindful activity could have served to achieve our results (for example, composing an opera, as Verdi did in his seventies). In either case, especially in light of all of the previous research discussed, the larger point is that some of the objectively measured, "irreversible" signs of aging were altered as a result of psychological intervention.[23]

The regular and "irreversible" cycles of aging that

we witness in the later stages of human life may be a *product* of certain assumptions about how one is supposed to grow old. If we didn't feel compelled to carry out these limiting mindsets, we might have a greater chance of replacing years of decline with years of growth and purpose.

CHAPTER 7

*

Creative Uncertainty

There's an old story about two men on a train. One of them, seeing some naked-looking sheep in a field, said, "Those sheep have just been sheared." The other looked a moment longer, and then said, "They seem to be— on this side." It is in such a cautious spirit that we should say whatever we have to say about the workings of the mind.
JOHN HOLT, *How Children Learn*

*

Had the rich stranger in Chapter 2 who needed a three-by-seven-foot piece of wood simply unhinged his own front door, observers of the scavenger hunt might have thought, "What a creative solution!" Many, if not all, of the qualities that make up a mindful attitude are characteristic of creative people. Those who can free themselves of old mindsets (like the man on the train), who can open themselves to new information and surprise, play with perspective and context, and focus on process rather than outcome are likely to be creative, whether they are scientists, artists, or cooks.

Mindfulness and Intuition

Generally, when creativity is being discussed, these mindful qualities come up under other names. Take intuition, for example. A scientist exercising intuition is very likely to be breaking loose from old mindsets and categories, or paying attention to the meaning of a surprise result.

Just as it is easier to get a grasp on mindfulness by first describing its opposite, intuition is most easily defined by comparing it to rational thought or logic. "It is by logic that we prove. It is by intuition that we discover," said the mathematician Henri Poincaré.[1] In dealing with the world rationally, we hold it constant, by means of categories formed in the past. Through intuition, on the other hand, we grasp the world as a whole, in flux.

Imagine trying to describe a brook. A running brook is never the same. New water flows past, working away, little by little, at the banks. From moment to moment it is a different brook. To talk about a brook we have to find a constant aspect of it. To perform any rational operation concerning the brook we must consider it unchanging, treat it as if it were the same. Language and rational processes both hold experience constant. To behave rationally, one uses categories formed in the past. "I'll meet you at the brook we went to yesterday." We can map its course as of today, measure its acidity at a certain point. Each time we treat it as the very same brook. An artist or writer, however, might choose not to hold it still but simply to experience the dynamic nature of the brook, to sit by it and become open to its "brookness." We call this approach mindful or intuitive; it bypasses old categories and rational thinking. The dancer Isadora Duncan, whose art is by definition motion and change, said, "If I could tell you what it meant, there would be no point in dancing it."[2]

Out of an intuitive experience of the world comes a continuous flow of novel distinctions. Purely rational understanding, on the other hand, serves to confirm old mindsets, rigid categories. Artists, who live in the same world as the rest of us, steer clear of these mindsets to make us see things anew. I recently attended a lecture by photographer Joel Meyerowitz. To my surprise his lecture was about mindfulness. He did not call it that, but to me his talk was a lesson in how to stay open to experience. When he spoke about the ocean, describing the way the light hit the undersides of the waves as they folded back into the sea, my old category of "wave" broke up into a throng of new impressions. I went back to the beach and looked for all kinds of waves, parts of waves, and patterns of waves.

Meyerowitz also described the amateur photographers who flock to the Grand Canyon. Arriving at the rim of this famous landmark, they shuffle about, searching for a sign that says "shoot here." With one pre-set image labeled GRAND CANYON in their minds, blinding them to what lies below, they search for the one and only "right" spot to stand. In advising his audience that there is no such spot and that they could search instead for whatever was "meaningful" to them,

Meyerowitz was encouraging a mindful approach applicable to far more than photography.

When our minds are set on one thing or on one way of doing things, mindlessly determined in the past, we blot out intuition and miss much of the present world around us. If Archimedes had had his mind set only on taking a bath, he probably would not have discovered the displacement of water. By keeping free of mindsets, even for a moment, we may be open to see clearly and deeply.

> While with an eye made quiet by the power
> of harmony, and the deep power of joy,
> We see into the life of things.

In these lines from *Tintern Abbey,* Wordsworth's quiet eye reflects another quality that links intuition and mindfulness. They are both relatively effortless. Both are reached by escaping the heavy, single-minded striving of most ordinary life.

Bach also spoke of the effortless flow of musical ideas. Asked how he found his melodies, he said, "The problem is not finding them, it's—when getting up in the morning and getting out of bed—not stepping on them."[3]

In an intuitive or mindful state, new information, like new melodies, is allowed into awareness. This new information can be full of surprise and does not always "make sense." If we resist, and evaluate it on rational grounds, we can silence a vital message. In the fall of 1941, during the blitz, Churchill, it is said, often went out late at night in a government car to visit anti-aircraft batteries. One night he was ready to leave a site, and an aide opened the back door on one side of his car. Churchill, however, walked around the car and let himself in the far door instead. Not long after that, a bomb exploded, nearly turning the car over. "It must have been my beef on that side that pulled it down," said Churchill. When his wife asked him why he had chosen to sit on the far side of the car, Churchill replied, "Something said to me, 'Stop,' before I reached the car door held open for me. It then appeared that I was told I was meant to open the door on the other side and get in and sit there—and that's what I did."[4]

We don't know if such episodes represent intuition—an attunement to information not perceived by most conscious minds—or merely coincidence. In any case, a respect for intuition and for the information that may come to us in unexplainable ways is an important part of any creative activity. "If man is to use his capacities to the full and with the confidence that fits his powers, he has no alternative but to recognize the importance and power of intuitive methods in all fields of inquiry—literature and mathematics, poetry and linguistics."[5]

Creativity and Conditional Learning

In Chapter 2 we saw how the teaching of facts as absolute truth can lead to mindlessness. A good deal of my research has explored the brighter side of the picture: the encouragement of creativity by teaching facts in a conditional manner. In most educational settings, the "facts" of the world are presented as unconditional truths, when they might better be seen as probability statements that are true in some contexts but not in others. What happens when this uncertainty is allowed in? Does the uncertain information become more available to us later, when the context has changed?

Alison Piper and I conducted some experiments to explore this question.[6] We introduced a collection of different objects which we identified to one group of subjects in an ordinary, unconditional way and to another in conditional terms. For instance, to the first group we said, "This is a hair dryer," "This is an extension cord," "This is a dog's chew toy." For the conditional group we just added the phrase "could be": "This could be a hair dryer," and so on, implicitly suggesting that under some circumstances the object might be seen in different ways. After the objects had all been introduced, we gave the subjects forms to fill out. In giving the instructions we deliberately made some errors. We then announced that we could not finish the study because the original forms were filled out wrong and we had no spare forms. In effect, we created an urgent need for an eraser to correct our mistake.

Since the dog's chew toy was an unfamiliar-looking piece of clean rubber, it filled the bill very nicely. However, only those subjects introduced to the toy conditionally thought to use it in this novel way.

What happens in people's heads when they learn that "this could be . . ."? Are they really learning conditionally, or are they instead saying to themselves that "could be" means "I don't know what it *is*, but maybe it is an X." Imagine reading a newspaper and spilling hot chocolate on it so that you can't make out a letter (it could be an *r* or an *n*); the choices are not unlimited. If this is what's going on, and people still have preconceptions of the item's identity, then our experiment, while still interesting, does not necessarily tell us how to promote an enduring kind of mindfulness. The experiment showed us that uncertainty resulted in more creative solutions than did certainty, not whether people could stay somewhat uncertain. To test this possibility, we ran a similar study, but with two important additions.

First, to the subjects who were introduced to objects in a conditional way, and those introduced in an absolute way, we added a third group whom we can call a "temporarily conditional" group. We introduced each object to them by saying, "I don't know what it *is* but it could be. . . ." Second, after we created an unusual need one of the objects could fill, we created another need. If people could learn about unfamiliar things in a truly conditional way, then they might see many different uses for the object. For example, another rubber object, a float for a toilet tank, was used as a ball and then as an eraser. The group that was told, "I don't know what it *is* but it could be a toilet float," thought to use the rubber object as a ball, but once they saw it as a ball most of them did so absolutely. That is, the identity of the object was no longer conditional. They did not think to use it in another novel way. Of course, neither did the absolute ("is") group.

The results for the group that met the object in a completely conditional way supported our prediction. At least twice as many people in this group, as in either of the other groups, thought of a way to fill the second need. It is as if this conditional group came to see that people create uses for objects. A use is not inherent in an object, independent of the people using it. The successful use of an object depends on the context of its use. (As an aside, it may be interesting to note that prices are created along with uses. When a scrap of rawhide or piece of rubber becomes a "dog's chew toy," its cost rises.)

Contrast this conditional way of learning with the way we usually learn. Take an orange juice can that has been washed out so there is not a trace of juice in it. Cover it with colored paper and fill it with pencils. To some this still *is* an orange juice can being used as a pencil holder. To those trained conditionally, it would, in its current context, be more a pencil holder than a juice can, though tomorrow it could be a vase.

Uncertainty may be more natural to some of us than others. Consider a person with dyslexia, for whom perceptual information is often distorted. He may not be sure, for example, whether a *d* seen on a printed page is really a *d* or perhaps a *b*. Individuals uncertain in this way might be less likely to take the world for granted and treat it mindlessly. To assess this we performed the same conditional/absolute experiment as before but now with dyslexic students as well as a control group of nondyslexic students. For half of each group the objects described above were presented conditionally, for the other half, unconditionally.

Once again, we found a more mindful or creative response from the normal conditional group than from the unconditional group. Most interesting, however, was the finding that dyslexic people tended to be more mindful even in the explicitly unconditional learning situation.[7] Of course this experiment demonstrated only one way in which teaching can be done in a conditional manner.

Teresa Amabile studied creativity in a group of preschool children.[8] The children were asked to make collages and were randomly assigned either to a group in which they were encouraged to choose the art materials they would be using, or to a group in which they would use materials chosen for them by the experimenter. After they had finished, judges who did not know which group was which found that the collages of students who selected their own materials were made more creatively.

These results could be explained in at least two ways. First, choice makes us feel more responsible for what we are doing; the children given the choice might have cared more and tried harder. Choosing materials— making comparisons—also forces us to draw mindful distinctions. It encourages a conditional view, a sense of possibility. For example, in choosing between two colors the child might think more of what can be done with a color than if he or she were simply given one color. In this way, choice encourages mindfulness.

Teaching can be done in a much more conditional way than just offering a choice of art materials. Children are usually taught "this is a pen," "this is a rose," "this is a car." It is assumed that the pen must be recognized as a pen so that a person can get on with the business of writing. It is also considered useful for the child to form the category "pen." But consider an alternative: What happens if we instruct the child that "this *could be* a pen"? This conditional statement, simple as it seems, is a radical departure from telling the child "this *is* a pen." What if a number of ordinary household objects were introduced to a child in a conditional way: "This could be a screwdriver, a fork, a sheet, a magnifying glass"? Would that child be more fit for survival on a desert island (when the fork and screwdriver could double as tent pegs for the sheet, near a fire made by the magnifying glass)? Or imagine the impact of a divorce on a child initially taught "a family is a mother, a father, and a child" versus "a family could be. . . ."

Some may argue that to teach children about the world conditionally is to make them insecure. This belief may result from a faulty comparison. If the world were stable and we taught stability, that might indeed be better than teaching conditionally. The appropriate comparison, however, would seem to be between teaching with absolutes when the "facts" are conditional versus teaching conditionally when the "facts" are conditional. Will children taught "it depends" grow up to be insecure adults? Or will they be more confident in a world of change than those of us brought up with absolutes?

Since childhood, I have eaten tuna fish salad. Until I was in my twenties, however, it never occurred to me, a middle-class New Yorker, that "tunafish" was a type of fish like any other, labelled "tuna." It never occurred to me that one might have substituted any other fish for tuna and have, for example, bluefish salad or swordfish salad instead. Of course, had I been asked "What are all the ways you could prepare bluefish?" I might have come up with bluefish salad. But the surprise I felt when I was first served fish salad that was not tuna made me feel foolish for not having realized sooner that tuna is just one of many fish. It also made me realize the strength of these mindsets. Even in the most minor and ordinary details of our lives, we are locked in by the unconditional way we learn in childhood. (I wonder what else I would know if only it occurred to me to ask.)

We pick up rules before we have a chance to question them. Is it "feed a cold and starve a fever," or "starve a cold and feed a fever"? I've been among adults arguing vehemently over this issue, without thinking of where this saying might have originated, or what current medical knowledge might have to say on the subject. If you learn something absolutely, it must be absolutely right. (In this case, both sayings could be right if what was originally meant was "If you feed a cold, you'll starve a fever" or "If you starve a cold, you'll feed a fever.")

One intriguing, if still tentative, connection between creativity and a degree of uncertainty in early experience can be found in a well-known 1961 study of the differences between creativity and intelligence. Jacob Getzels and Philip Jackson gave a group of schoolchildren a conventional IQ test and another test designed to measure "creativity."[9] This latter test measured five kinds of ability: (1) word association—students were asked to give as many definitions as possible to common stimulus words (such as *bolt, bark*); (2) finding different possible uses for things—how many ways to use a brick, for example: as a foot warmer, a weapon, a paperweight, for building, as a step, for a bookcase, as a fulcrum, as a source of red powder; (3) finding hidden shapes in complex geometric forms; (4) fables—students were required to provide "moralistic," "humorous," and "sad" endings to each of four fables; (5) making up problems—students were required to make up as many mathematical problems as could be solved with information given in written paragraphs. Success on all these tasks was measured by the number, novelty, and variety of responses. (The advantages of a conditional education on tests of this sort may be readily apparent.)

Getzels and Jackson then compared the backgrounds of those who had scored highest on the "creativity" test with those whose IQ scores were highest. They found that parents of the high IQ group tended to have higher educational status. The mothers of this group were more stereotypic in descriptions they gave of themselves, much more class-conscious and more concerned with financial status and security. In terms of our discussion of mindfulness, these mothers appeared to have more rigid mindsets. The highly creative subjects' mothers described their families in more global/emotional terms, used more rounded descriptions, and seemed to have felt much less personally concerned with finances in their own background, whatever their situation. Particularly interesting in terms of our discussion of creativity and conditional learning is the investigators' observation that the mothers of the highly creative group showed many more uncertainties about their own child-training practices.

Getzels and Jackson's study suggests a link between intelligence as measured by IQ tests and conformity to the norms of the culture and its institutions: family, school, occupational field, and so forth. The background of the more creative students seemed to allow for more nonconformity. Some of the students deemed the most highly creative were actually described as non-conformists. This observation is borne out by our studies of mindfulness and deviance described in Chapter 8.

After we reach college, we encounter teaching done in a conditional manner. We are taught about *theories, models, hypotheses*, and not just "facts." Theories and the like are implicitly conditional and explicitly statements of uncertainty, at least by definition and at least for the moment. Later they may become laws. Nevertheless, we have found that if a theoretical model is presented absolutely, it will be thought absolute and the student may thereafter treat it rigidly.

In 1986, Jennifer Joss and I tested the effect on students of presenting a theoretical model in absolute or conditional terms.[10] Undergraduates from Harvard and Stanford were given a written lesson on urban development. The lesson concerned the way city neighborhoods evolve. For three separate, randomly chosen groups of students, the lesson was written in three different ways: (1) in absolute terms; (2) in a conditional way, using terms such as "could be," and "may be"; (3) in absolute terms but *introduced* as "one possible model" for neighborhood evolution.

All the subjects were asked to read the lesson and complete the test following it. In the test there were first some questions designed to make sure that all three groups were receiving the same information. This was important, to assure that the differences found were the result of the way the information was processed and not the content of the information. The rest of the test measured the students' ability to use the information presented. Once again, groups who received it in absolute terms were less able to put the information to creative use. They were not mindful enough to notice when a made-up case did not fit the model at all. Even Group 3 (for whom the content of the lesson was clearly identified as conditional—"one possible model"—but the presentation was still absolute) was less able to make spontaneous use of the information.[11]

The dampening of creativity in students by unconditional teaching is compounded by most textbooks. Scientific investigations yield only probability statements and not absolute facts. And yet, these probabilistic data and information that are true only under certain circumstances are presented in textbooks as though they were certain and context-free. Harvard paleontologist and writer Stephen Jay Gould has criticized what he calls the "internal cloning of text to text."[12] In an amusing article he traces the comparison of one of the early ancestors of the horse, *Eohippus*, to a fox terrier. At the turn of the century (when fox terriers were very popular) fossil evidence suggested that these horses were similar in size to the fox terrier. The comparison was made again and again and is still repeated in current textbooks. The more it appears, the more it is likely to be perceived as an unconditional fact. (After all, how can you argue with what *everyone* knows to be true?) Since these little "dawn horses" are now believed by sophisticated paleontologists to have weighed over fifty pounds, the venerable simile to a terrier less than half this weight may be mindless and outdated. (Of course, we should remember that fifty pounds is also an estimate.)

Distinctions and Analogies

Since "creativity" and "mindfulness" may be two ways of looking at many of the same qualities of mind, there is no end to the parallels that could be made between them. One in particular may be when we look in later chapters at the implications of mindfulness research in the workplace, for an understanding of prejudice, and for healing and health.

Students of the creative process have long distinguished between two kinds of thinking: analysis and synthesis. Sometimes the Latin word *cogito*, meaning "I think" in the sense of analyzing or taking apart, is contrasted with *intelligo*, meaning "I understand" in the sense of gaining insight into the nature of something.[13] J. P. Guilford has examined the mental abilities involved in creativity, using a similar distinction.[14] On the one hand, there is the generation of new information from old information—"divergent production"—and on the other, there are abilities of "redefinition" or "transformation" of thought.

To put these contrasting kinds of thought more simply: We can look at the world and ask how things differ (make distinctions) or how they are the same (make analogies). The first approach results in the creation of new categories, the second usually involves shifting contexts, both of which we have described as mindful activities. We have discussed the mindful nature of novel distinction-making at some length. Thinking by analogy is equally important to both mindfulness and creativity.

The ability to make or spot analogies has long been of interest to people who try to judge intelligence. Candidates for graduate work in certain fields, for instance, must take an exam called the Miller Analogies Test, which contains multiple-choice questions such as the following:

> *Lion* is to *Pride* as *Horse* is to: (circle one)
> Vanity   Herd   Corral[15]

In making an analogy, we apply a concept learned in one context to another one. Such a mental operation is in itself mindful. Architects who can see how one setting, say, a hospital, resembles another, say, a hotel, can come up with designs more responsive to complex needs. Intentionally mixing metaphors with an eye toward finding similarities can spark new insights. Comparing people, businesses, and religions, across and within categories, for example, can lead to a greater understanding of both sides of the comparison. How is Pete like a library / a library like a train / a train like a restaurant?[16]

Jean Piaget wrote that his work on the child's conception of time, motion, and speed was inspired by Albert Einstein's work in the domain of physics and relativity. "Einstein," wrote Piaget, "once suggested that we study the question from the psychological viewpoint and try to discover if there existed an intuition of speed independent of time." According to the physicist Gerald Holton, one of Einstein's many contributions was to generate ideas that lent themselves to "further adaptation and transformation in the imagination of similarly exalted spirits who live on the other side of disciplinary boundaries."[17]

This ability to transcend context is the essence of mindfulness and central to creativity in any field.

CHAPTER 8

*

Mindfulness on the Job

The supreme accomplishment is to blur the line
between work and play.
ARNOLD TOYNBEE

*

The ability to shift contexts may be just as valuable to
a manager or on the assembly line as it is to an artist
or physicist. Fatigue, conflict, and burnout can all result
from being mired in old categories, trapped by old
mindsets. In fact, virtually all the advantages of mindfulness described in the earlier chapters can be found
in the workplace. For employer and employee alike,
mindfulness may increase flexibility, productivity, innovation, leadership ability, and satisfaction. Since most
of us, almost all day, almost all week, are either traveling
to work, working, worrying about work, or planning
the work ahead, the applications of mindfulness to the
work setting are particularly useful.

Welcoming the Glitch

An old Vedic proverb admonishes, "Avert the danger not yet arisen." To catch the early warnings of trouble, we must be alert to new information, to subtle deviations from the way things typically go. In the office study described in Chapter 2, a memo was circulated that said only, "Return this memo immediately." Most of those who received it did not notice its absurdity. Because it was in most respects similar to memos they saw every day, they mindlessly returned it. From this we can see how larger problems can result from initially small, unnoticed changes. When mindful, people tend to notice such problems before they become serious and dangerously costly. Whether it is a slight shift on a dial in a nuclear energy plant, or the first hint of what Theodore Levitt of the Harvard Business School calls the "shadow of obsolescence,"[1] the early signs of change are warnings and, to the mindful, opportunities.

The workplace is full of unexpected stumbling blocks that can get in the way of productivity. To a mindful manager or employee, these become building blocks. They don't impede progress because they are seen as part of an ongoing process, rather than disastrous deviations from past procedure. Take a situation in which instead of the usual four people "required" to do a job, only three turn up, or one in which a piece of equipment routinely used in production is down for the week. If the employees in that department are locked in old mindsets, the work will come to a screeching halt. A mindful employee, oriented to the present, might reassess the job as one for three people, or for whatever equipment was at hand. Deviations from some habitual way of working are less problematic if there is tolerance for uncertainty and no rigidly set method in the first place. The "deviations" then become simply elements of the present situation.

Second Wind

As we saw with the Coolidge Effect described in Chapter 3, fatigue and satiation do not necessarily occur at fixed points. To a large extent, mental and physical exhaustion may be determined by premature cognitive commitments; in other words, unquestioned expectations dictate when our energy will run out.

As far back as 1928, psychologist Anita Karsten studied situations that at first feel good, but with repetition become neutral or uncomfortable.[2] She put subjects in "semi-free situations" in which they were given tasks to do but were instructed that they could stop working whenever they were tired. They were told to do the work as long as they enjoyed it. Tasks were of two types: continuous activities such as drawing, and tasks that come to a quick end but are repeated, such as reading a short poem again and again. (Tasks like chess that are long but come to an end were not used.)

For each type of task, the subjects worked until they grew weary. The investigator then changed the context. For instance, after the subjects had drawn until exhausted, the investigator asked them to turn the page over and re-draw the last picture they had drawn, to show the experimenter how *fast* they could draw it. The "totally exhausted" subjects had no difficulty repeating the drawing in the new context. Another subject was given the task of writing *ababab* . . . until he had had enough. He went on until he was mentally and physically exhausted. His hand felt numb, as though it couldn't move to make even one more mark. At that moment the investigator asked him to sign his name and address for a different purpose. He did so quite easily. He was not feigning exhaustion. Rather, the change of context brought renewed energy.

When Karsten had subjects read poems aloud, after a while they became hoarse. When they complained to her how they hated the task, however, the hoarseness disappeared. Similarly, another subject, who claimed to be so fatigued that she could no longer lift her arm to make even one more hatch mark, was then seen casually lifting her arm to fix her hair.

New energy in a new context is known to most people as a "second wind." We see examples of it daily. Take a harried young scholar who has been working all day writing a book, while also taking care of his rambunctious two-year-old daughter. By the time his wife comes home to help, he is too exhausted to move. But just then a call comes from a friend asking if he would like to play basketball. He leaps up and dashes off to play for four hours.

In each of these cases, a mindset of fatigue was lifted by a shift in context initiated by someone else—

the investigator or a friend. Mindful individuals use the phenomenon of second wind to their own advantage in a more deliberate way. Staggering different kinds of paperwork, changing to a different work setting, and taking a break to jog or make a phone call are all ways to tap latent energy by shaking free of the mindset of exhaustion. (Mindfulness in itself is exhilarating, never tiring.) A self-starting, autonomous employee can do it for herself; a mindful manager can make it happen for others. The challenge for management is to introduce context changes within the required work load.

Another kind of mindset that can lead to fatigue is the way we define a task. When we begin any undertaking, we have a mental picture of its beginning, middle, and end. In the beginning we tend to be energetic and mindful. In the middle phase, we may perform the task mindlessly or mindfully. If we are performing it mindfully, we are involved in creating new distinctions while we do it. We do not have a sense of ourselves as separate from the task. The task may seem effortless as long as we are involved in process and distinctions are being created. If we do the task mindlessly, we rely on distinctions already made. As the task nears its end, we typically become focused on outcome and also expect fatigue to occur. We now notice the task as separate from ourselves as we evaluate the outcome. When we near the end of activities that we expect to be tiring, fatigue arrives. This mental picture of the end of a task is a self-imposed context and makes fatigue almost inevitable. Changing contexts *before* reaching this point may prevent fatigue. A simple change of activity will not necessarily bring this about, however. The change must be *experienced* as a new context. If a new physical exercise, for example, is still seen as exercise, the expectation of fatigue in that context may remain.

In an interesting study psychologists Janice Kelly and Joseph McGrath had subjects perform various tasks either under severe time constraints or with plenty of time. If the first task had to be completed in a hurry, there was plenty of time for the second and vice versa. Subjects apparently made a premature cognitive commitment to the requirements of the first task. When no longer under time pressure, subjects became unnecessarily fatigued, performing as though still under the clock.[3]

Innovation

Changing of contexts, as we've seen in earlier chapters, generates imagination and creativity as well as new energy. When applied to problem solving, it is often called *reframing*. A young musician recently told me of his long-standing inability to finish the songs he composed. This had bothered him deeply, and he felt like a failure as a composer until he reframed his "problem." Rather than seeing himself as incapable of finishing a song, he realized what a great gift he had for composing new themes. He then teamed up with someone who is great with musical detail and together they are highly prolific.

Changing contexts is only one path to innovation. Creating new categories, exploring multiple perspectives, and focusing on process all increase the possibility that a novel approach to a problem will be discovered. A tolerance for uncertainty on the part of management is also encouraging. If a manager can risk deviation from routine ways of doing things, creative employees can thrive and contribute. If not compelled only to make a product better and better, they may find ways to make a different, better product.

The imaginative use of "outsiders" can encourage each of the types of mindfulness just mentioned.[4] A man or two in an all-female company, a teenage board member, or a blind retiree can bring in new ideas. Independent consultants can fill the same role. Creating the position of outsider in a company, regardless of the characteristics of the person hired to fill it, can keep important questions flowing. Just as a traveler to a foreign culture notices what people indigenous to that culture take for granted, an outsider in a company may notice when the corporate natives are following what may now be irrational traditions or destructive myths. When routines of work are not familiar, they cannot be taken for granted and mindfulness is stimulated.

In *Getting to Yes*, Roger Fisher and William Urey suggest ways that negotiators can generate within their own minds the kind of perspectives brought by outsiders from different disciplines: "If you are negotiating a business contract, invent options that might occur to a banker, an inventor, a labor leader, a speculator in real estate, a stockbroker, an economist, a tax expert, or a socialist."[5] This openness to multiple perspectives—an essential ingredient in mindfulness—supports a policy of workers switching responsibilities, or switching career midstream. If the switch is within a field, rather than across fields, the benefits of a fresh perspective can outweigh the problems of having to learn a new technical jargon. For example, if an art historian became a vision psychologist, or vice versa, each might have something different to bring to the question, "How is a three-dimensional object rendered in two dimensions?"

Distance from the mindsets of an industry is vital in designing products. Take a company that makes wheelchairs. Now that the elderly population is increasing, so should their business. Some people come to need wheelchairs the way others come to need eyeglasses. But unlike eyeglasses, wheelchairs have looked the same for years. There is no reason, other than habit, that wheelchairs must look so medical and ominous. Designers are now beginning to see wheelchairs as racing cars, as recreational vehicles, as colorful, comfortable, and zippy ways to get about. Eight years ago, in a nursing home where I consulted, we had residents decorate their own wheelchairs to make them more appealing and/or functional. The very word *wheelchair* seemed to take on a different flavor after this project. Just recently, I came across advertisements for the "Wildcat," the "Palmer 3," and the "Turbo"—three sleek new designs that seem to redefine what being in a wheelchair means.

As pointed out earlier, innovation can be dampened by too narrow an image of the task. People who make wheelchairs could see themselves in the transportation business or the recreation business in order to break out of the mindsets associated with handicaps and hospitals. Theodore Levitt, whose famous phrase "marketing myopia" could be translated into "mindless marketing," came up with a delightfully poignant example of obsolescent mindsets: the buggy whip industry. While one could argue that no amount of product innovation could have saved this business, a new self-definition might have: "Even if it had only defined its business as providing a stimulant or catalyst to an energy source, it might have survived by becoming a manufacturer of, say, fanbelts or air cleaners."[6]

Narrow definitions of competition go hand-in-hand with narrow mindsets about a product. Small banks, for instance, see themselves in competition with other small banks, in the role of collectors and lenders of money to and from their communities. A bank like Citibank, which saw its function as an "information-processing activity," was able to compete much more powerfully. In the same way, the maker of Royal or Remington or Smith Corona typewriters would not have found their real competition by looking at one another. Over in another corner, a division of IBM was gearing up to knock them out of the running with the Selectric typewriter. This was a totally new concept for producing words on paper, later to be supplanted by the personal computer and word processors in all their forms.

One way to escape narrow definitions is to con-

sider the actor/observer difference. A student made me
aware of a good example of this in government. At the
end of every fiscal period, agencies and researchers
given government monies rush to spend whatever
money that remains in their budgets rather than return
unspent money to the government. They've used what
they needed and now waste the rest. From a taxpayer's
perspective, this seems irrational. Why squander the
money rather than return it to be used by others? The
reason is that if the agencies do not spend the money,
their budgets for the next fiscal year will be reduced—
"They didn't need it last year so they probably don't
need it this year either," frugal officials would say. And
so agency after agency wastes money to keep future
budgets healthy. The clever solution that my former
student, Otto Brodtrick, suggested, based on his au-
diting experience for a Canadian government agency,
took into account the point of view of those receiving
the funds. If each year an agency's budget were guar-
anteed to be what it would have been had it spent all
the money given, plus half of what it did not spend,
both individual agency and government would prosper.
For instance, if the agency were given $10,000 and
spent only $8,000, it would get $10,000 the next year
plus half of what it saved ($1,000), for a total of
$11,000. The following year, if, of the $11,000 it spent
only $10,000, it would get $11,500 the next year. Both
sides would end up winning. Future budgets would be
healthy and current spending would be sensible. The
agency or researcher would be pleased to return rather

than waste money not needed in the present because of the guarantee of more money in the future.

The Power of Uncertainty for Managers

Employee behavior, mindless or innovative, is not likely to be independent of a manager's style. Of all the qualities in a manager conducive to innovation and initiative, a degree of *uncertainty* may be the most powerful. If a manager is confident but uncertain—confident that the job will get done but without being certain of exactly the best way of doing it—employees are likely to have more room to be creative, alert, and self-starting. When working for confident but uncertain leaders, we are less likely to feign knowledge or hide mistakes, practices that can be costly to a company. Instead, we are likely to think, "If he's not sure, I guess I don't have to be right 100 percent of the time," and risk taking becomes less risky. Employees are more likely to suggest process and product changes that could be beneficial. Admission of uncertainty leads to a search for more information, and with more information there may be more options.

Debra Heffernan, a doctoral student at Harvard, and I conducted research that looked at the power of uncertainty in an organizational setting.[7] We evaluated the degree of certainty of managers in the organization by asking them, among other questions, how many of the decisions they make each day have absolute correct answers. We also assessed their general level of confidence. Questionnaires were given to employees to assess their work relationships with the managers. We found that those managers who were confident but relatively uncertain were evaluated by their employees as more likely to allow independent judgment and a general freedom of action.

Because people perceived as bright and knowledgeable tend to become managers, the sense that the boss knows *the* answer is pervasive and asking questions is potentially intimidating to employees. If managers make clear that they see certainty as foolhardy, it is easier to ask questions based on one's own uncertainty. Questions provide a good deal of information for managers. Moreover, if managers seek out information from employees to answer these questions, both will probably become more mindful and innovative.

Ironically, although work may often be accomplished mindlessly, with a sense of certainty, play is almost always mindful. People take risks and involve themselves in their play. Imagine making play feel routine; it would not be playful. In play, there is no reason not to take some risks. In fact, without risk, the pleasures of mastery would disappear. Imagine mindlessly skiing or horseback riding; imagine going to the theater to see the same old play without searching for a new twist; imagine doing crossword puzzles already done, to which you remember all the answers. We tend to be more adventurous at play because it feels safe. We stop evaluating ourselves. Play may be taken seriously, but it is the play and not ourselves that we are taking seriously—or else it is not really play at all. It would seem, then, that to encourage mindfulness at work, we should make the office a place where ideas may be played with, where questions are encouraged, and where "an unlucky toss of the dice" does not mean getting fired.

Many managers, however, become anxious when faced with a question for which there are no easy answers. When challenged with a question about the rationale for a policy, they reach for the ready-made replies that we all learned in childhood: "Do it because I told you to." In organizations, a very familiar mindset is evident in the reply: "What if we let everybody do that?" Many innovative ideas have probably been squelched by that phrase. If only a few want to do something (whatever the "it" is), what difference does it make? If everyone in fact wants to do it, perhaps it should be done. At a nursing home where I consulted, an elderly woman wanted to make a peanut butter sandwich in the kitchenette instead of going to the dining room for dinner. The director said, "What if everyone wanted to do that?" If everyone did, the nursing home might save a lot of money on food. At the very least, it would have been useful information for the chef.

Should deviant procedures that occur only once in a while be tolerated? Should unanimous desires for change lead to a new policy? Such questions may be important for any organization. Answers like, "What if everyone wanted to?" or "We've never done it that way

MINDFULNESS

before," turn an opportunity for innovation into a dead end.

In the academic world, where certainty and scientific proof are much prized, the need to acknowledge uncertainty is valued but still often fiercely resisted. One day I arrived late for the meeting of a committee formed to award a teaching prize, only to find my colleagues upset, confronted with an "impossible" moral dilemma. The problem they faced was that there were five nominees for the prize and only three to five letters of recommendation for each. How could we make a sensible decision based on so little evidence? The question at first seemed reasonable. However, the rather unkind way the committee came down on the person in charge of gathering the nomination materials made me think twice about it. They pointed a finger at her as though she had violated some absolute unwritten rule. With three to five letters the award would be "arbitrary." There should be more information; everyone agreed. But what does "more information" mean? What would be conclusive evidence of teaching skill? Should the letters be from students who currently are taking the course, or those who just finished it? If they were taught well enough maybe the lesson should still influence them after the course is over; perhaps the letter should be from people who took the course two years ago. Or should it be five years ago? Should the letters be from the good students, the poor students, or all the students? One could make a reasonable argument for each. Or should letters be from students at all? Colleagues know what goes into teaching in the first place. What

146

about some combination such as half of each, two faculty to every one student asked, and so on?

When I tuned back in to the meeting, I suggested that since the decision about how many and what kind of recommendations could never be based on "enough information," we should go ahead and award a prize this year and for future years make an *arbitrary* but explicit rule of thumb to follow. Instead of an endless search for certainty and mountains of paper, an arbitrary rule allows any committee, in academia or a corporation, to get on with a decision. By remembering that this rule was simply an agreement, the construction of one committee, however, one is more willing to change it when circumstances change without having to attack those who came up with it. Rules are best to guide, not to dictate.

Besides a quality of confident uncertainty, there is another quality of leadership that is well known but harder to define. Charisma in leaders has a magical aura, which may account for the belief that leaders are born and not made. In a recent investigation conducted with John Sviokla of the Harvard Business School, I tried to explore an aspect of charisma that may be linked to the power in uncertainty and mindfulness.[8]

We first looked at charisma in a theatrical setting. Actors who were performing in plays around the Harvard campus, such as *The Importance of Being Earnest*, *Miss Julie*, *The Merchant of Venice*, were randomly assigned to two groups. Those in one group were instructed to perform their parts in as novel a way as possible, varying it within the realm of the character.

Those in the other group were asked to perform their parts as consistently with the script as possible. After the play, the members of the audience, unaware of our instructions to the actors, were handed a brief questionnaire to rate the actors' charisma. Those actors instructed to perform in a novel way were rated as more charismatic.

To investigate this phenomenon further, in another setting, we gave encyclopedia salespeople instructions similar to those we gave the actors. One group was instructed to approach each new prospect as if he or she were their very first customer. Though they stuck to the "script," they subtly adapted their approach as needed. The other group was told to be as consistent in their approach as possible: "The more consistent you are, the higher your sales will be." The first group of salespeople was seen as significantly more charismatic than the second. Curiously, they were also seen by customers as more knowledgeable about their product, even though this knowledge did not vary among the salespeople. They approached each customer in a more flexible manner, and their pitch had more impact. A certain open-mindedness would seem to enhance powers of persuasion as well as charisma.

Burnout and Control

Burnout, a problem in a wide variety of workplaces from emergency rooms to corporations, is compounded by mindlessness. Rigid mindsets, narrow perspectives, the trap of old categories, and an outcome orientation all make burnout more likely. Conversely, as we have seen, changing contexts and mindsets, or focusing on process, can be energy-begetting.

Many of us know the energizing effects of a new job. There is an excitement in learning new things, mapping out a new territory. As the job becomes familiar, however, enthusiasm and energy wane. Burnout sets in when two conditions prevail: Certainties start to characterize the workday, and demands of the job make workers lose a sense of control. If, in addition, an organization is characterized by rigid rules, problems that arise feel insurmountable because creative problem-solving seems too risky. When bureaucratic work settings are of the "we've always done it this way" mentality, burnout is no stranger.

In medical settings, where errors may cost lives, these conditions are especially characteristic. Debra Heffernan and I tried to combat burnout in Stevens Hall Nursing Home in North Andover, Massachusetts.[9] We introduced the staff to ideas of uncertainty and control so as to make them more mindful. We demonstrated that the "facts" they used to guide their care-giving were really probabilities and not certainties. We had meeting after meeting in which we questioned how they could be so sure of the rationale behind their policies. We paid particular attention to those mindsets that may induce dependency in the residents and rob them of control. For example, a blind elderly resident wanted to smoke. This was burdensome to the staff, who felt he must be accompanied to prevent him from burning down the establishment. Their solution had been to allow him to smoke only two cigarettes a day. But how could they be sure that he needed help? Another patient's disease made it hard for her to brush her hair. When a member of the staff brushed it for her, he or she was unwittingly implying that she could not do it for herself. One of the more dramatic cases was a woman who couldn't remember to go to the dining room. The staff felt they had to escort her so that she wouldn't starve. These cumulative and seemingly relentless responsibilities, seen as essential, contributed to feelings of burnout.

Once the staff understood that their justification for these solutions were much weaker than they had thought, they were able to find other ways of solving the problems. By returning some control to the residents, they made their own jobs easier. For example, they came to realize that there was no firm reason to believe that a blind man couldn't learn to smoke safely. In fact, he already knew where and how to smoke without danger. They just had to give him a chance. The woman who had trouble brushing her hair was happier doing it herself as long as she approached the task in very small, incremental steps. And no one starved. Her hunger helped the forgetful woman remember where the dining room was. Seeing that problems may be solvable without relying on old rules made the staff feel more in control; seeking solutions made them more mindful. Records comparing the period before our intervention and a similar period of time afterward showed that staff turnover was reduced by a third. Less feeling of burnout meant less reason to leave. These results, though not experimentally derived, suggest that burnout is not inevitable. In a recent experimental investigation conducted at Lewis Bay Head Injury Facility, we offered the nurses and other caregivers a similar kind of mindfulness training. With the resultant change of outlook, and a renewed sense that new solutions were possible, the staff in this demanding and potentially depressing situation showed a significant increase in morale and job satisfaction.

This kind of "care for the caregiver," restoring a feeling of control and options, may become more and more important in hospitals. Nursing shortages, pressures resulting from cost containment, legal constraints, and technical complexity all contribute to increased stress on staff. In a report from a committee at the Harvard Medical School set up to study fatigue in residency training, the reduced length of stay for hospitalized patients ("quick-in and quick-out") was seen as a cause of increased exhaustion among residents. When patients are discharged prematurely, and evaluated by other doctors before they are admitted, the resident loses a sense of control over the case, seeing his or her role as purely mechanical. A lack of mindful involvement in the patient's recovery is clearly implicated in this kind of burnout. In fact, the faculty recommendations included ways of restoring the "cognitive and intellectual function in the management of the patient," that is, mindfulness.

Since the world of work confronts us with the same puzzles that face us in the rest of our lives, these observations about the effects of mindfulness on the job could become a book in themselves. It is probably also clear to readers familiar with business and management that the more progressive thinkers in this field have long been aware of the dangers of fixed mindsets and outcome orientation and the advantages of multiple perspectives and shifting context, but under other labels. In the 1920s, Mary Parker Follett, a pioneer in management studies, anticipated certain of these ideas, emphasizing especially the value of a shift in mindsets. Follett's warnings about an obsession with outcome are pertinent for any manager today: "A system built round a purpose is dead before it is born. Purpose unfolds and reflects the means."[10]

Certainty tends to develop with continued success. There is a tendency to continue doing whatever has worked, ironically making successful businesses more vulnerable to petrified mindsets. I spent part of a recent sabbatical at the Harvard Business School, where colleagues helped me streamline some of the ideas in this chapter. Some of us even made a game out of considering desk plaques for executives:

"Mindlessness is the application of yesterday's business solutions to today's problems."

"Mindfulness is attunement to today's demands to avoid tomorrow's difficulties."

CHAPTER 9

*

Decreasing Prejudice by Increasing Discrimination

"If I am a plaything for you giants, be gentle with me. . . ."

"Come!" said she, accepting the offer of my hand to help her over the fender, and looking wistfully up into my face, "you wouldn't mistrust me if I was a full-sized woman."

I felt that there was much truth in this; and I felt rather ashamed of myself.

"You are a fine young man," she said, nodding. "Take a word of advice, even from a three foot nothing. Try not to associate bodily defects with mental, my good friend, except for a solid reason."

CHARLES DICKENS, *David Copperfield*

*

David Copperfield is having a lesson in discrimination. By distinguishing between mental and physical defects, he will avoid discriminating against people of short stature. Distinctions that are specific rather than global can be very useful in breaking down the mindsets of prejudice.

Most attempts to combat prejudice have been aimed at reducing our tendency to categorize other people. These efforts are based on the view that, in an ideal world, everyone should be considered equal, falling under the single category of "human being." Yet categorizing is a fundamental and natural human activity.[1] It is the way we come to know the world. Any attempt to eliminate bias by attempting to eliminate the perception of differences may be doomed to fail. We will not surrender our categories easily. When we cease (for whatever reason) to make any particular distinction among people, we will probably make another.

An understanding of the nature of mindfulness suggests a different approach to combating prejudice— one in which we learn to make more, rather than fewer, distinctions among people. If we keep in mind the importance of context and the existence of multiple perspectives, we see that the perception of skills and handicaps changes constantly, depending on the situation and the vantage point of the observer. Such awareness prevents us from regarding a handicap as a person's identity. Instead of a "cripple" or a "diabetic" or an "epileptic," we would see a man with a lame leg, a woman with diabetes, or an adolescent with seizures. These distinctions become more useful when further refined, for example: a person with 70 percent hearing instead of a deaf person, someone with non-insulin-dependent diabetes instead of diabetes.

A Patient by Any Other Name

Most of our labels for people tend to be global: genius, midget, homosexual, giant. Such labels tend to influence every other judgment of, or reaction to, the person who bears them. I first came to notice this effect when I was a clinical intern in the psychology department at Yale. When people walked in the door of the clinic, they labeled themselves "patients," and at the time I saw them this way as well. When we discussed certain behaviors or feelings that they saw as a problem, I also tended to see whatever they reported as abnormal. I saw their behavior as consistent with the label of patient. Later, outside of the therapy context, when I encountered exactly the same behavior (for example, difficulty in making a decision or in making a commitment) or feelings (like guilt or the fear of failure) in people whom I know, it appeared to be perfectly common or to make sense given the circumstances. To test the impact of labels, Yale psychologist Robert Abelson and I designed an experiment using a videotape of a rather ordinary-looking man being interviewed.[2] He and the interviewer sat in armchairs facing each other and talked about work. We showed this videotape to psychotherapists. For half of the therapists, we called the man being interviewed a "job applicant." For the remaining half, we called him a "patient." The therapists to whom we showed the tape were of two different backgrounds. Half had been trained in various traditional ways; the training of the other half had specifically emphasized the avoidance of labels.

We found that when we called the man on the tape a job applicant, he was perceived by both groups of therapists to be well adjusted. When he was labeled a patient, therapists trained to avoid the use of labels still saw him as well adjusted. Many of the other therapists, on the other hand, saw him as having serious psychological problems.

Because most of us grow up and spend our time with people like ourselves, we tend to assume uniformities and commonalities. When confronted with someone who is clearly different in one specific way, we drop that assumption and instead look for more differences. Often these perceived differences bear no logical relation to the observable difference. For instance, because of the unusual gestures of a person with cerebral palsy, we might assume a difference in intelligence. Such faulty assumptions tend to exaggerate the perceived gap between "deviants" and "normal people." In the following passage from *Gulliver's Travels*, we can see this process taking place as Gulliver watches some "strange creatures."

Their shape was very singular, and deformed, which a little discomposed me, so that I lay down behind a thicket to observe them better. Some of them coming forward near the place where I lay, gave me an opportunity of distinctively making out form. Their heads and breasts were covered with thick hair, some frizzled and other lank; they had beards like goats, and a long ridge of hair down their backs, and the fore parts of their legs and feet; but the rest of their bodies were bare, so that I might see their skins, which were of a brown buff color. They had no tails, nor nay hair at all on their buttocks, except about the *anus*; which, I presume, nature had placed there to defend them as they sat on the ground, for this posture they used as well as lying down, and often stood on their hind feet.[3]

When we observe the people around us as we go about each day, so many details escape us: slight tics, gestures, features such as moles, spaces between the teeth, and the like. When face to face with someone who is different, however, we tend to notice these details or quirks. Because we do not typically notice them, the various traits we notice in someone perceived as "deviant" will be seen as extreme or unusual.

In another study, conducted at Harvard, a video-tape was shown to three groups of students.[4] For the first group, the person on the tape was given one of several labels: a millionaire, a homosexual, an ex-mental patient, a divorcé, or a cancer victim. The second group of students watched the video without being given a label for the person on the tape. This group was composed of students who were instructed to attend to and think about the tape that they would see. The third group just watched the video monitor without instructions, as if watching TV. The viewers in the first and second groups, whether or not they had been given a label for the man they were watching, saw him more accurately than did the third group. When tested, they recalled more of his physical characteristics correctly. In fact, when we later showed slides of several different people, including the person on the tape either as he was or "doctored up" (with glasses and a mustache), the first two groups recognized him. Both the deviant label and the instructions to pay attention made them more mindful. The third group did not recognize him.

Despite this accuracy in recognition, the two mindful groups (label and no label) evaluated the characteristics of the person on the tape as extreme. They judged him to be different from most people they know. The third group simply "saw" the person on the tape as normal and ordinary. From the results of this study, we can see that the presence of a person labeled as deviant makes us more mindful (that is, we notice specific details) but also reveals how mindless we generally are. The traits and details that we pick up when mindful are taken to be unusual or extreme. If we use these mindfully collected observations to justify biased mindsets, prejudice is reinforced.

The Painted Cast

The mindful curiosity generated by an encounter with someone who is different, which can lead to exaggerated perceptions of strangeness, can also bring us closer to that person if channeled differently. A most undramatic little incident that happened many years ago in New Haven made this effect clear to me. I was walking to the supermarket and noticed a young woman approaching from the opposite direction. She had a heavy cast on her leg, which I looked at as we passed. We exchanged friendly smiles and I paused to wonder why our interaction left me with pleasant feelings. I had not felt any awkwardness when I looked at her large cast. The cast had been colorfully decorated, inviting me or anyone else to stare at it and thus to think about it. My curiosity had been made legitimate.

When I discussed this little incident with colleagues, we came up with a hypothesis to explain why we avoid encounters with people who are physically different and also how this effect can be overcome. People stare at novel stimuli. When the novel stimulus is a person, however, it is culturally unacceptable to stare. Therefore, we reasoned, people may avoid those who are different in an effort to avoid the conflict between wanting to stare and feeling it inappropriate to do so. The painted cast resolved this conflict; people were invited to stare. With no conflict, there was no avoidance. (As I now understand it, novel stimuli provoke mindfulness. When the context of that mindfulness is not taboo, interactions may proceed smoothly.)

To test this hypothesis we designed an experiment.[5] Subjects were asked to sit in a waiting room where they would later meet a partner pre-selected by us. This woman, whom the subject had never met, either wore a leg brace, was pregnant, or had no striking characteristic. A glass partition in the room looked out into another waiting room. We casually explained to subjects that this was an experimental room and that from the other side of this partition was a one-way mirror. The partner entered the other waiting room and the subject could see the partner without being witnessed in return. The subject, thus, could stare without embarrassment until the novel stimulus was familiar. For half of the subjects the curtain on the mirror was drawn so that they could not look at their partners surreptitiously. All subjects waited in the first room under the assumption that the experiment had not yet begun.

After a certain time, we introduced the subjects to their partners and observed their reactions. Those who did not view the partner before meeting her acted more distant when she was either in a leg brace or pregnant. For example, they chose to sit farther away from her than from the "normal" partner. Thus far, of course, this was not an unusual finding. People tend to avoid people who are "deviant." In contrast, however, when subjects viewed the person ahead of time and sated their curiosity, they did not sit away from the pregnant or disabled person or show other signs of avoidance. This rather straightforward experiment suggests many ways in which encounters with people seen as different (for instance, in schools where handicapped children are "mainstreamed") can be enhanced by providing an outlet for mindful curiosity.

Mindfully Different

As we saw in the last chapter, being an outsider in a company or other situation can increase mindfulness. A disability or deviant label of any kind can have the same effect, leading a person to question the shared mindsets of the group.

Dyslexia, as we saw in Chapter 7, can have the effect of maintaining in the afflicted person a certain level of mindfulness. Because people with dyslexia often do not see letters and numbers in the same way that others do, they may not take other "accepted facts" for granted. In carrying out schoolwork, dyslexic children may not trust themselves to process information mindlessly, because they are not sure they have it right in the first place. Learning for these children thus becomes more conditional, a mode that, as we pointed out earlier, is potentially conducive to greater creativity.[6]

Sensory as well as physical handicaps create a series of hurdles that require mindful solutions. The deaf, blind, or wheelchair-bound person must approach simple activities, that others pursue mindlessly, in a more problem-solving frame of mind. Hadi Madjid, a blind, Harvard-trained economist, writes of the continuous puzzles confronted by the handicapped person. For instance, of wanting to go skiing with his friends. He figured that by attaching bells to the poles of the skier just ahead, he could learn to weave his way down a trail.[7] Stephen Hawking, the very distinguished British physicist, has learned to master one complex communication device after another (such as a keyboard that produces artificial speech) as he keeps one step ahead of the neurological disease that has paralyzed most of his muscles and left him unable to speak.

Ironically, the greater mindfulness generated by a handicap, or other difference, can create yet one more way in which the person differs from the majority. Greater mindfulness may lead to original perceptions that others may view as bizarre. These perceptions often may be more informed (that is, may result from noticing more distinctions about the world). In combating prejudice, then, the issue is not simply how we might teach the majority to be less judgmental, but also how we might all learn to value a "disabled" or "deviant" person's more creative perceptions.

When those who are considered deviant find no support for their original views of the world, they often join others who are similar, to affirm their perceptions. Paradoxically, this may not foster continued mindfulness. Consciousness-raising that leads to shared mind-sets rather than to continued questioning may actually promote mindlessness. When taught that it is okay to be old, black, gay, disabled, divorced, a recovering alcoholic, and so on, people may become less likely to question their perceptions, including those in areas unrelated to their different status or level of ability.

While a mindful view of the world may come more naturally to a disabled person, this may not extend to his or her own handicap. A mindless assumption of limitations associated with particular handicaps may in itself be disabling. This kind of mindlessness, which lowers the expectations of a handicapped person, can arise as a protection for that person's self-esteem. The disability is used as a justification for failure or poor performance. Such excuses are useful to all of us. Individuals without disabilities frequently employ "self-handicapping" strategies, building in explanations for possible failures.[8] For example, people might drink or avoid studying much before an exam so as to feel that if they hadn't been drinking or had studied, they would have done well. These fabricated explanations are more apt to have the flavor of a rationalization than the more compelling, "real" handicap of the deviant.

Consider, for instance, two teenage girls who both love to ride horses and are learning to jump. One of the girls has inherited a condition called albinism, which can cause poor eyesight. The two girls ride equally well, and one day they ride out to practice jumping. The riding teacher keeps raising the jump. Finally, it becomes so high that neither girl can get over it; their horses refuse.

As they ride back, the "normal" girl is berating herself endlessly, whereas the albino girl is not so hard on herself. Because of her condition, for better or worse, she did not have the same rigid expectations. People with disabilities may be protected from the negative effects of failure by lower expectations of success. If someone with a disability and someone without it confront a new task and fail (and that failure is perceived by both performers to reflect low ability), the person with a disability may be better protected from a drop in self-esteem. That same protection, however, may hold a disabled person back, insofar as low expectations undermine performance.[9]

In a society for which outcome rather than process is of primary value[10] (by our definition, a more mindless society), deviance and disability are much more apt to lower self-esteem. For instance, a deaf student who is constantly comparing his comprehension of the lectures against that of his classmates who are not hearing-impaired might feel demoralized. The same student concentrating instead on mastering the subtleties of lipreading might feel highly encouraged. In fact, in a society concerned primarily with process, the notion of deviance might have much less, if any, significance.

Disabling Mindsets

Unless we grow up with a handicapped person in the family, most of us first learn about handicaps as something not relevant to our lives. Mindless stereotypes (premature cognitive commitments) may be uncritically accepted. If the issue later becomes relevant, these mindsets may be hard to shake. For instance, what happens to people who become handicapped through an accident? They may become victims of their own mindsets. If, for example, they had mindlessly accepted a relationship between physical and mental handicaps, they may worry unnecessarily that their mental faculties have been impaired as well. If a handicap becomes relevant to us not through personal injury but rather through injury to a close relative, a child, for example, the old stereotypes may affect that relationship. A parent who had once picked up an antiquated image of a "village idiot" might respond to a deaf-mute child as if he or she were mentally deficient.

These global stereotypes also prevent us from taking advantage of the talents around us. If the school football team needed to plan better strategies against a competitor, for instance, and the best person to help was a certain superb football strategist, she might not be asked because she sits in a wheelchair. If you with-hold your vote from a politician because he is gay, overlook a surgeon because she is a woman, a psychi-atrist because he is blind, or a potential consultant because she has only one arm, you may miss out on the most qualified person.

The very definition of *deviance* may of course be misleading in the first place. Earlier we mentioned that any categorical distinction can be broken down into further distinctions. Once we are aware of these dis-tinctions and make enough of them, it may no longer be possible to view the world in terms of large polarized categories such as black and white, normal and disabled, gay and straight. With skin color, this difficulty is pretty obvious. But take the distinction between homosexuals and heterosexuals. These categories do not seem to overlap; there are people who prefer sexual behavior with their own sex and they are called homosexuals, and there are people who engage in sexual behavior with members of the opposite sex and they are called heterosexuals. Surely this is clear.

The bisexual who enjoys sex with both genders is the first obvious exception to this distinction. Next, where do we put a man who prefers to fantasize about men while making love to women? Then, what about a completely celibate person; or the married transves-tite; or the person who makes love with a transsexual presently of the opposite sex; or the person who was heterosexual, had one homosexual experience, and is now without a partner? To continue this just a bit longer, where do we put the so-called heterosexual couple, or for that matter homosexual couple, who no longer makes love? This is not a small group of people.

If the categories "heterosexual" and "homosexual" apply exclusively to sexual activity, then during the time people are not making love, they might be classified either way. We could call them heterosexual if their last encounter was heterosexual; homosexual, if their last encounter was homosexual. If the majority of their sexual experience was heterosexual, however, perhaps we should consider them heterosexual. But what if the best of these experiences were homosexual? And so on. Moreover, if one's definition of sexuality were based on the nature of the behavior, rather than with whom it took place, what sense would it make to label couples "gay" or "straight" if they engaged in all the same behavior? Consider where we would put a man who is impotent but still tries to satisfy his wife or a woman who enjoys foreplay but not intercourse.

For even more obvious reasons it makes no sense to speak of physically handicapped people as a category. Describing particular activities for which a person with a particular disability might be less competent reduces the global quality of the handicap label and thus, as we said before, makes it only an aspect of that person instead of a whole identity. This mindful perspective should reduce the importance of deviance for both actor and observer, for we would soon see that we are all "handicapped." Deviance as a category relies for its definition on another category, "normal," with which it is mutually exclusive. To define "normal" necessitates evaluative judgments. To be a "paraplegic" or a "diabetic," or to be "too fat" or "too thin," suggests that there is one ideal way to be a human being. To be "deviant" means that one does not belong to this so-called "normal" group. In itself, the notion of deviance has no meaning.

Discrimination Without Prejudice

A mindful outlook recognizes that we are all deviant from the majority with respect to some of our attributes, and also that each attribute or skill lies on a continuum. Such an awareness leads to *more* categorizing and consequently fewer global stereotypes, or, as we said earlier, increasing discrimination can reduce prejudice.

To test the effect of increasing mindful distinctions on the perception of deviance, Richard Bashner, Benzion Chanowitz, and I conducted an experiment in a local elementary school.[11] We tried to find out whether encouraging children to make distinctions actively would teach them that handicaps are task- and context-specific. Children were shown slides of people and then given a questionnaire relating the people shown with different kinds of skills. For the experimental group, we asked for several answers to each question on the questionnaire. For the control group, we asked for only one answer to each question.

Most of us are brought up to find *the* answer rather than *an* answer to questions. We do not easily come up with several alternatives. By requiring that the children in the first group give several different answers to each question, we were also requiring them to draw mindful new distinctions. The group that gave one answer (albeit a different one for each slide) was not exercising this capacity. Our general hypothesis was that training in mindfulness would result in less *indiscriminate* discrimination.

One of the slides, for example, pictured a woman who was a cook. She was identified as deaf. The experimental group was asked to write down four reasons why she might be good at her profession and four reasons why she might be bad. The control group was asked to list one good and one bad reason. This group was asked six additional questions requiring only one answer in order to keep the number of answers constant. Several questions were asked of this kind about different professions.

A second part of this training in discrimination presented problem situations and asked the children "how" they might be solved. They were to list as many ways as they could think of (experimental group), or they were simply asked whether they could be solved (control group). For instance, when viewing a woman in a wheelchair they were either asked in detail *how* this person could drive a car or simply asked, *Can* this person drive a car?

A third exercise in making distinctions involved finding explanations for events. We gave the children a slide and a short written description of what was happening (for instance, a girl spilling coffee in a lunchroom). The experimental group was told to think up several different explanations for the situation while the control group again considered only one explanation. The number of explanations required for each set of questions increased throughout the training for the experimental group. The same number of slides was presented to every child.

After all this "training" the children were given several tests to assess prejudice. One was a measure of general disability discrimination. They were shown slides of children with and without various handicaps and were asked to indicate whom they wanted on their team for activities such as checkers, soccer, a singalong, a tug of war, a wheelchair race, a game of Frisbee, seesawing, and pinning the tail on the donkey. We chose handicaps and activities so that nonhandicapped children would be more suited for some activities, handicapped children for others, and for some activities it would not matter. For example, experience in a wheelchair would be helpful for the wheelchair race just as blindness would not hinder performance on pin the tail on the donkey. However, neither would be especially helpful in a game of soccer, and for a singalong these handicaps would be irrelevant.

Our results showed that children can be taught that handicaps are function-specific and not person-specific. Those given training in making mindful distinctions learned to be discriminating without prejudice. This group was also less likely than the control group to avoid a handicapped person. In essence, the children were taught that attributes are relative and not absolute, that whether or not something is a disability depends on the context. Such a mindful view of disabilities may be a valuable asset as these children grow up and move into that large category of people that our society sees as disabled, the elderly—or, on the way, join the category of "patient."

CHAPTER 10

*

Minding Matters:
Mindfulness and Health

Is there a split between mind and body, and if so, which
is it better to have?
WOODY ALLEN, *Getting Even*

*

From earliest childhood we learn to see mind and body
as separate and unquestioningly to regard the body as
more important. We learn that "sticks and stones may
break your bones, but words can never hurt you." If
something is wrong with our bodies we go to one kind
of doctor, while with a "mental problem" we go to
another. Long before we have any reason to question
it, the split is ingrained into us in endless ways. It is
one of our strongest mindsets, a dangerous premature
cognitive commitment.

Mind and body have not always been seen as separate, however. There have been periods of history and
cultures in which this dualism was not an assumption.
Sir Charles Sherrington, speaking of Aristotle's concept
of mind, points out that the "impression left by *De*

Anima is Aristotle's complete assurance that the body and its thinking are just one existence . . . the oneness of the living body and its mind together seems to underlie the whole description."[1] Today among the !Kung, a people of the Kalahari Desert of southern Africa, healing practices for physical and psychological disturbances are the same. Their all-night healing dances are performed to treat problems ranging from marital troubles to coughs to insufficient breast milk. The healing energy of the community is focused on the whole person, not just on a disease or body part.[2]

As we saw in the discussion of entropy in Chapter 3, many scientists, such as James Jeans and Arthur Eddington, have questioned the view of the universe as a great machine, a purely physical reality. "Throughout the physical universe runs that unknown continent which surely must be the stuff of our consciousness,"[3] wrote Eddington. In psychology, however, a dualistic view has been persistent. Since, until the end of the last century, psychology as a discipline was considered a branch of philosophy, psychologists' notions of mind were derived from those held by philosophers. The separation of mind and body is traced by many historians to Descartes, who saw the mind as nonmaterial and the body as material. Only the body was subject to mechanical laws. Though many later thinkers have quarreled with this view, it persisted for a long time in psychology and still persists in the way most of us look at ourselves.

Behaviorists such as Watson and Skinner challenged this view earlier in this century and argued that behavior could be understood by focusing only on that which can be observed, including the antecedents to and the consequences of behavior. Early behaviorism held that behavior had environmental or situational, but not mental, causes. In this school of thought, life can be described without reference to mental events; there are only physical stimuli and physical responses. Mind is viewed as an empty construct, an epiphenomenon.

Until the 1950s the choice for psychologists lay between dualism or behaviorism. The language of dualism prevailed. Even among those who were studying only behavior, there remained, in life away from the lab at least, an implicit acknowledgment of the mind/body distinction. Today, much of the focus in psychology has shifted to the study of cognition. While the word *cognition* is synonymous with mental activity, research in this field is designed so that tests of cognition and cognitive processes are behavioral. In the newer field of neuroscience, dualism seems to have resurfaced as a mind/brain distinction.

Dualism: A Dangerous Mindset

All this would be a matter of semantics or academic philosophy were it not for the fact that a rigid view of mind as separate from body has serious consequences. Among the most extreme of these consequences is the phenomenon of "psychological death." The patient mentioned in Chapter 4, who improved when moved to a more hopeful ward and died when moved back to the "hopeless" ward, shows that distinctions between physical and mental illness are questionable. The "failure to thrive" syndrome, seen in institutions where babies are given adequate physical care but not enough cuddling and stimulation, is another consequence of ignoring the interdependence of physical and mental health.

A related kind of dualism, also with potential to harm, is the distinction between thought and feeling (cognition and affect). Although cognition is generally seen as necessary in order to experience emotion,[4] some psychologists, including William James[5], have viewed emotion as a purely bodily state. Visceral change, in this view, *is* the emotion.[6] Robert Zajonc, at the University of Michigan, has argued that one does not need cognition in order to experience affect.[7] He has shown that when subjects are presented with tones that they had, albeit unwittingly, heard before and others they had never heard, subjects preferred the familiar tone sequences even though they couldn't discriminate between the two on the basis of familiarity. Here feeling seems to precede thought. Though they did not know they had heard them before, they liked them more.

Neither separating these two functions, nor trying to reduce one to the other, seems to me to make sense. Nor is it enough to see them as simply related. Viewing them instead as part of one total simultaneous reaction, a reaction that may be measured in many different ways, may be more clarifying. For instance, an intelligence test could be seen as a measure of the individual's emotional well-being at the moment the test was given as well as an evaluation of IQ.

For a stimulus to be emotionally provocative it first has to be thought of in some form. To fear a lion is to think of a lion fearingly; to admire a horse is to think admiringly of a horse; and so on. The thought and the physical reaction to it co-occur. To see something one has to distinguish it from something else. To hear something, the same is true. A figure can be experienced only against some background. Because perception is a constructive process, the same form in different contexts yields different stimuli. Thus a lion seen in a cage in a zoo, or in a circus ring, is not frightening. The "same" lion, seen from the same distance in your backyard, for example, is likely to be terrifying. If the lion is fear-provoking in one context and not in another, then before fear can be experienced, one has to supply the fearful context.

Contexts are learned. Thus most of what provokes emotion is learned. And these emotional contexts are generally learned in a single-minded way. Children are not taught that the way they feel in a particular context could be either fear or delight. Instead children are taught that snakes are frightening, sunsets are peaceful, mothers (and motherlike people) are loving. Emotions rest upon premature cognitive commitments. We experience them without an awareness that they could be otherwise, without an awareness that this is the way we, albeit passively, constructed the experience. If someone or something contradicts the "truth" of these emotional associations to which we have committed ourselves, we point out that they (feel right.) Since they feel right, they are true. But they may feel right simply because of the way they were originally learned, just as a tune first heard a certain way sounds wrong if played differently later.

Without looking closely and noticing that the same stimulus in different contexts is a different stimulus, we become victims of the associations we ourselves constructed. When we are tormented by unwanted emotions, we assume it could be no other way.

The Body in Context

An integrated view of thought and emotion makes it possible to understand the importance of context for our health and well-being. Take the fear we feel when a doctor orders a biopsy as a cancer-screening measure. In some cases, a tiny breast lump or a mole requires an incision no larger than is needed to remove a bad splinter. But our fear is based upon our *interpretation* of what the doctor is doing, not simply the procedure. Our thoughts create the context which determines our feelings. In thinking about health, and especially in trying to change the impact of illness or the behavior that leads to it, an understanding of context is vital.

When we think of various influences on our health, we think of many of them as coming from the outside environment. But each outside influence is mediated by context. The response of our bodies does not reflect a one-to-one correspondence to stimuli in the external world because there is no one-to-one correspondence between the external world and how we perceive it. Any stimulus can be seen as simultaneously many stimuli. Our perceptions and interpretations influence the way our bodies respond. *When the "mind" is in a context, the "body" is necessarily also in that context.* To achieve a different physiological state, sometimes what we need to do is to place the mind in another context.

The power of context to affect the body may be considerable, even to the point of influencing basic needs. In an experiment on hunger, subjects who chose to fast for a prolonged time for personal reasons tended to be less hungry than subjects who fasted for extrinsic reasons (in this case, because of the scientific value of the experiment and a payment of $25).[8] A fee or other extrinsic reason to undertake a difficult task may not change the way we feel about the task. Freely choosing to perform that task, however, means that one has adopted a certain attitude toward it. In the experiment, those who had made a personal (psychological commitment) to fasting reported less hunger. They also showed less of an increase in free fatty acid levels, a physiological indicator of hunger. Thus, the different state of mind meant a different state for the body.

The effect of context on pain has been known for a long time. In *The Principles of Psychology*, William James describes a Dr. Carpenter who suffered severe neuralgia:

He has frequently begun a lecture while suffering neuralgic pain so severe as to make him apprehend that he would find it impossible to proceed; yet no sooner has he by a determined effort fairly launched himself into the stream of thought, than he has found himself continuously borne along without the least distraction, until the end had come, and the attention has been released; then the pain has recurred with a force that has overmastered all resistance making him wonder how he could have ceased to feel it.[9]

When one can take one's mind off pain, it seems to go away. Conversely, when the mind returns to pain, so does the body. If one can reinterpret a painful stimulus, it may cease to be painful. The results of this strategy may be more lasting than simply distracting the mind since, once the stimulus is reinterpreted, the mind is unlikely to return to the original interpretation. In Chapter 5 we saw how patients can learn to tolerate pain by seeing it in a different context (thinking of bruises incurred during a football game, or cutting oneself while rushing to prepare for a dinner party). This mindful exercise helped them use fewer pain relievers and sedatives and leave the hospital earlier than other patients matched for comparison.

Henry Knowles Beecher compared the frequency of pain severe enough to require medication in soldiers wounded in World War II and in a matched group of civilians.[10] Although the soldiers had extensive wounds, only 32 percent required medication, compared to 83 percent of the civilians. Robert Ulrich reported that gall-bladder-surgery patients who had been assigned to hospital rooms with windows facing brilliantly colored fall trees had shorter postoperative stays and took fewer pain relievers than those assigned to rooms that faced a brick wall.[11]

Part of the hospital context is its strangeness. But seen in a different way, this unfamiliarity may disappear. Hospital staff, after all, are people, windows are windows, and beds are beds. And yet we let this perceived strangeness have a great impact on us. In a dramatic investigation, K. Järvinen studied patients who had suffered severe heart attacks and found that they were five times as likely to experience sudden death when unfamiliar staff made the rounds than would be expected in any comparable time period. However, the strangeness did not reside in the staff. Novelties and familiarity are qualities we impart to the environment.[12] Had patients been helped to see the way these staff members were like people they already knew and cared for—thereby making them less unfamiliar—the consequences might have been different.[13]

Context can influence even the acuity of our senses. This may be seen in a study of vision, which I undertook together with several student colleagues at Harvard.[14] We made use of the belief held by many people that pilots have excellent vision. Our subjects were students in R.O.T.C. They were asked to imagine themselves as air force pilots—that is, they were told to try to *be* pilots, rather than thinking of acting a part. Our hypothesis was that their eyes would match what their minds believed pilots' vision to be. One of the investigators, Mark Dillon, was in R.O.T.C. and was able to arrange use of a flight simulator. Our subjects got into uniforms and, with instructions, "flew" the simulator, an activity that very closely mimics actual flying. A comparison group also got into uniform, but for them the simulator was broken so that they had to simulate the simulation.

No mention of vision was made. At the start of the study, before the pilot context was introduced, subjects were given a short general physical in which a test of vision was included. While flying (or pretending to fly, depending on the group), subjects were asked to read the markings on the wing of a plane that could be seen out the cockpit window. These "markings" were actually letters from an eye chart. Although the findings need further replication, vision improved for approximately 40 percent of the subjects when they were in the pilot context, while no one improved in the comparison group. When other groups were added, designed to control for arousal and motivation, the results remained basically unchanged.

Context affects the physiology of animals as well as people. Chronic overcrowding of rats, especially during growth and development, may result in heavier adrenal and pituitary glands.[15] Another study suggests that the difference found in cortical weight and thickness between rats reared in enriched environments versus those in isolated environments persists for as long as the rats live in these different social settings.[16] Many other studies by neuroscientists have shown similar anatomical changes resulting from psychological influences.

A wide body of recent research has been devoted

to investigating the influence of attitudes on the immune system. The immune system is thought to be the intermediary between psychological states and physical illness. The emotional context, that is to say, our interpretation of the events around us, would thus be the first link in a chain leading to serious illness. Richard Totman, a British clinical psychologist, describes one of the possible "psychosomatic" chains of events:

Psychological states, through their impact on the higher centre of the brain and the limbic-hypothalamic-pituitary-adrenal pathway, could tip some of the sensitive balances which govern the body's response to a vast number of diseases in which the immune system is involved. These range from infections and allergies to arthritis, auto-immune diseases and cancer, and include numerous other degenerative complaints associated with ageing. There would thus seem to be no shortage of potential "ways in" for psychological influences in the causation of such conditions.[17]

Since context is something over which we have control, the continuing clarification of these links between psychological states and illness is good news. Diseases thought to be purely physiological and incurable may be more amenable to individual control than we have believed in the past.

Even when the course of a disease may appear to progress inexorably, our reactions to it can be mindful or mindless and change its impact on us. A very common mindset, for example, is the conviction that cancer means death. Even if the tumor has not yet had an effect on any body function, rarely will one think of oneself as healthy after having a malignancy diagnosed. At the same time, there are almost certainly people walking around with undiagnosed cancer who consider themselves healthy. Many doctors have observed that after a diagnosis of cancer, patients seem to go into a decline that has little to do with the actual course of the disease. They appear, in a sense, to "turn their faces to the wall," and begin to die.

Addiction in Context

While alcoholism and drug addiction are often seen as intractable problems, very difficult to treat, the importance of context in both conditions leaves room for optimism. For instance, even the degree of intoxication can be changed by changing the drinker's expectations. In one experiment, researchers divided a group of subjects according to whether they *expected* to receive an alcoholic (vodka and tonic) or a nonalcoholic (tonic) drink. Subjects were told that they were taking part in a taste-testing contest and were instructed to sample the liquids ad-lib and rate them. Despite the presumed physiological effects of the drug on behavior, expectations were the major influence. What the subjects expected determined how much they drank, how aggressively they behaved, and in general how intoxicated they seemed.[18] In a similar study, investigators found that the groups of men who believed they had been given alcohol, whether or not the belief was true, showed a tendency for reduced heart rate.[19]

These are just a few of the many investigations showing that thoughts may be a more potent determinant of the physiological reactions believed to be alcohol-related than the actual chemical properties of alcohol. The antics of high school kids at parties, generation after generation, are probably also influenced by context just as much as by the quantity of beer consumed. As we've seen in Chapter 3, we all grow up with firm premature cognitive commitments regarding how alcohol affects behavior. These mindsets are potent influences on the role alcohol plays in our later lives.

Drug counselors have observed that heroin addicts are less likely to report withdrawal if they don't consider themselves addicts. Those who take the same amount of heroin and call themselves addicts often suffer much greater withdrawal symptoms. Informal reports from people who work with heroin addicts show that those addicts who are sent to prisons having the reputation of being "clean" (that is, where they believe there is absolutely no chance they will be able to get drugs) do not seem to suffer intense withdrawal symptoms, while addicts in other facilities who are denied the drug but believe they might be able to get their hands on it do experience the pain of withdrawal. Out of mind, out of body.

The strong effect of context on addiction can also be seen in work with Vietnam veterans. In a study carried out by Lee Robbins and colleagues, soldiers who had a drug problem while serving in Vietnam were compared with a similar group of addicts who had picked up the habit nearer to home. The veterans may have taken up drugs to handle the acute stress of war. Since this external justification was left behind in Vietnam, so was their perceived need for the drugs.[20]

An even more dramatic effect of context has been reported in relation to drug overdose.[21] As experience with drugs such as opiates increases, a tolerance builds up. Users progress to doses that would have been fatal earlier. Many users die, however, from a dose that should *not* be fatal to them. Shepard Siegel and some fellow researchers have suggested that the failure of tolerance on the day of the overdose is a function of context. In an experiment with rats they found that if a large dose of a drug is given in the presence of cues that are associated with sublethal doses, the rats were more likely to survive than those given the same dose in a situation not associated with the drug at an earlier time. The tolerance of both groups of rats was lowered when the drug was given in an unfamiliar environment. Siegel and his colleagues conclude: "Identical pretest pharmacological histories do not necessarily result in the display of equivalent tolerance to the lethal effect of heroin." In each study they ran, those in the strange testing situations were more likely to die of an "overdose than those in the familiar situation."

If context can change not only the severity of withdrawal symptoms but even the effect of a drug overdose, addiction may be more controllable than is commonly believed. For, unlike rats, human beings can change both the situational context (for example, putting ourselves in a familiar or drug-free environment or seeing the familiar in the seemingly unfamiliar environment) and, more important, the emotional context (the meaning of the addiction).

We all know people who have stopped smoking "cold turkey." Are they successful because their commitment to stop puts withdrawal symptoms into a new context? For many years I stopped smoking from time to time, found it too difficult, and began again, as so many people do. When I stopped the last time, almost ten years ago, I felt no withdrawal symptoms. There was no will power involved; I simply did not have an urge to smoke. Where did it go?

Jonathan Margolis and I explored this question in two stages. First we tried to find out whether smokers in a nonsmoking context experienced strong cravings.[22] We questioned smokers in three situations: in a movie theater, at work, and on a religious holiday. In the lobby of a movie theater that prohibits smoking while inside the theater, we approached people who were smoking and asked if we could question them briefly during the film and again on their way out but before lighting up their cigarettes. In the work setting we tested subjects in situations where smoking was prohibited, and also before or after a break, when it was allowed. Finally, Orthodox Jews, prohibited from smoking on the Sabbath by their religion, were questioned during and immediately after the holy day. The results in each setting were very similar. People did not suffer withdrawal symptoms when in any of the nonsmoking contexts. Returning to a context where smoking was allowed, however, their cravings resurfaced.

All these subjects escaped the urge to smoke in a

mindless manner. Could they have achieved the same thing deliberately? "I can resist everything except temptation," says a character in Oscar Wilde's *Lady Windermere's Fan*. Our question here is: Can people control the experience of temptation?

In designing the second experiment to answer this question, Jonathan and I assumed that a mindful addict would look at the addiction from more than one perspective.[23] From an open-minded position, it is clear that there are advantages as well as disadvantages to addictions. Though perhaps obvious, this is not the usual point of view for someone trying to break a habit or addiction. People who want to stop smoking, for example, generally examine only the negative consequences of smoking. They remind themselves of the health risks, the bad smell, other people's reactions to the smoke, and so on. But when they smoke, people are not thinking of the health risks or the smell, so trying to stop because of these reasons often results in failure. Part of the reason they fail is that all the *positive* aspects of the addiction still have a strong appeal. The relaxation, the taste, the sociable quality of stopping for a cigarette remain tempting. A more mindful approach would be to look carefully at all these pleasures and to find other ways of obtaining them. If the needs served by an addiction can be served in other ways, it should be easier to shake.

To test whether this dual perspective was at work when people quit smoking, Jonathan and I tried an indirect tactic. We picked a group of subjects who had already quit and complimented each one for having succeeded. We then paid careful attention to whether they accepted the compliments. To understand our strategy, imagine being complimented for being able to spell three-letter words. A compliment does not mean much when the task is very easy. If you solve a horrendously difficult problem, on the other hand, a compliment is probably most welcome. We then asked the same subjects what factors they considered when they decided to stop smoking. Those who gave single-minded answers, citing only the negative consequences, were more likely to be the ones who had accepted the compliment. Those who saw both sides usually shrugged it off. Months later we got in touch with people in the study to see if they were still nonsmokers. Of those we could reach, the subjects who had considered positive aspects of smoking and fended off the compliments were more likely to have been successful in quitting.

This work opens up some interesting questions for addiction research and therapy. While recognizing the positive reasons for the addiction and finding substitutes is not easy, the attempt to do so may help us find more mindful ways of breaking destructive habits.

The Traditional Placebo: Fooling the Mind

A well-known technique for helping us control those functions of the body not previously thought to be under conscious control is biofeedback. In the 1960s it became clear that intentional control of one's "involuntary" internal systems such as heart rate, blood flow, and brain waves was possible with the aid of biofeedback equipment. This equipment monitors the internal processes and makes them visible to patients on various kinds of dials and measuring devices. In this way it provides feedback for patients as they try to affect the working of their own bodies. Through trial and error, "involuntary" responses seem to come under a person's control. In the years since biofeedback was first demonstrated, researchers like myself have asked why these external devices are necessary. Why must people look to biofeedback machines for feedback rather than to internal cues? In other words, can we train ourselves to become mindful of processes within our own bodies?

Another method of harnessing the healing powers of the body in an indirect or passive way is the use of placebos. As commonly used a placebo is an inert substance, prepared to resemble an active drug and given to patients in experiments so as to have a basis of comparison for the results of that drug. Most such experiments are "double-blind," meaning that neither the investigator nor the patient knows who is receiving the drug and who is receiving the placebo. Usually the placebos have an effect as well, and the difference in degree between this effect and that of the drug is taken as a measure of the drug's effectiveness. For a drug to be marketed, it must outperform the placebo. If the investigators find no difference between real pills and placebos, they are led to believe that the physical medication was ineffective. There is room for question here, however, because placebos can have powerful effects. In fact, a considerable part of the effect of most pre- scriptions is considered to be a placebo effect. A well- known quip about new drugs warns doctors to use them as soon and as often as possible, while they still have the power to heal.

When patients are given a placebo and then get well, the illness is considered to be "only psychologi- cal." (Here we see the old mind/body dualism, alive and well.) It is interesting that no one tests the effec- tiveness of active drugs by telling patients that "this is only a placebo." (Is this implicit recognition of the power of the mind to change the effect of the drug?)

Despite great interest in placebos, no one yet knows exactly how they work. In an effort to explore this, investigators have used "placebo" treatments to change the immune system of rats. One remarkable study asked how long the lives of rats genetically pre- disposed to a disease called *systemic lupus erythematosus* could be extended with a placebo treatment.[24] In this "autoimmune" disease, the immune system turns on the body itself. One group of rats received a weekly injection of a drug that suppressed the immune reac- tion, immediately after being given a new liquid to drink. A second group received the same treatment, the drug and the new liquid, but an inert injection was substituted for the drug half the time. Thus, this second group received only half the total amount of the drug received by the first. The third group was identical to the second, except that the injections and new liquid to drink were not paired, but given on different days.

Finally, a control group of rats was given the new drink once a week, together with an inert injection. This group never received the immunosuppressive drug.

The critical comparison, for our purposes, is between the second and third groups. If the disease developed more slowly in the second group than the third, the rats were somehow suppressing their own immune systems in a way that could not be attributed to the drug. This is precisely what was found. The mortality rate of the second group was significantly lower. The mortality rate of the third group, in fact, was the same as that of the control group. Also striking was the fact that the mortality rates for the first and second groups were almost the same, even though the first group received twice the amount of the active drug. The power of the placebo to produce a strong effect on the immune system was dramatically confirmed.

Placebo effects are real and powerful. Who is doing the healing when one takes a placebo? Why can't we just say to our minds, "repair this ailing body"? Why must we fool our minds in order to enlist our own powers of self-healing? Placebos, hypnosis, autosuggestion, faith healing, visualization, positive thinking, biofeedback are among the many ways we have learned to invoke these powers. Each can be seen as a device for changing mindsets, enabling us to move from an unhealthy to a healthy context. The more we can learn about how to accomplish this mindfully and deliberately, rather than having to rely on these elaborate, indirect strategies, the more control we will gain over our own health.

The Active Placebo:
Enlisting the Mind

In several of the healing practices just mentioned, the role of the individual in bringing about change is by no means passive. An intentional effort to change an unhealthy mindset or a premature cognitive commitment is evident. Take hypnosis, for instance. Most contemporary writers on the subject agree that hypnosis cannot take place without the compliance of the subject. Some go so far as to say that all hypnosis is self-hypnosis.[25]

The treatment of warts makes a graphic illustration of this self-healing power. Believed to be caused by viral invasion, warts qualify as a "real" physical condition: they are visible, touchable, and lasting. Yet they respond to hypnosis. As the biologist Lewis Thomas wrote in *The Medusa and the Snail*, "warts can be made to go away by something that can only be called thinking or something like thinking. . . . It is one of the great mystifications of Science: warts can be ordered off the skin by hypnotic suggestion."[26]

Thomas goes on to describe one of several experiments where a group of subjects was given a hypnotic suggestion to be rid of warts and another group, control subjects, was not given these instructions. Of the experimental group, nine out of fourteen successfully got rid of the warts compared to none in the control group. Thomas points out how difficult it would be to accomplish this without the wisdom of the body. One would have to be a "cell biologist of world class" to know what orders to send out to eliminate the wart. Yet the experimental subjects who removed their warts were average educated individuals.

Another dramatic experiment with warts reveals how very specific our orders to the body can be. Fourteen subjects under hypnosis were asked to rid themselves of warts, but only on one side of their bodies. Nine of these subjects were able to bring about this result, becoming completely free of warts on that side.[27]

Despite the part we play in the healing that takes place under hypnosis, the process still feels somewhat passive. What are the ways we can work on our health more actively? First of all, we have to regain the control taken away by the experience of consulting an "expert" in a mindless fashion. Ever since we relied on our mothers to make a bruised knee better with a Band-Aid and a kiss, we have held on to the assumption that someone out there, somewhere, can make us better. If we go to a specialist and are given the Latin name for our problem, and a prescription, this old mindset is reconfirmed. But what if we get the Latin name without the prescription? Imagine going to the doctor for some aches and pains and being told that you have *Zapalitis* and that little can be done for this condition. Before you were told it was Zapalitis you paid attention to each symptom in a mindful way and did what you could to feel better. Now, however, you have been told that nothing can be done. So you do nothing. Your motivation to do something about the aches, to listen to your body, is thwarted by a label.

In the past decade or so, a new brand of empowered patient/consumer has tried to restore our control over our own health. Many of the alternative therapies sought out by these patients have as their active ingredient increased mindfulness. For instance, Carl Simonton has worked for years to erase the mindset of cancer as a death sentence. He believes that cancer is often a symptom of difficulties in a person's life. "The cancer patient has typically responded to these problems and stresses with a deep sense of hopelessness, or 'giving up.'"[28] This emotional response, Simonton believes, begins to set off physiological responses that suppress the body's natural defenses, which in turn make the body susceptible to producing abnormal cells. The Simonton technique for helping cancer patients involves active imagination on the part of the patient. The patient is to visualize the cancer and visualize the "good" cells in the body, or the chemotherapy or radiation, destroying the cancer. In order to participate in this process, the patient must exchange the mindset of cancer as a killer for that of the tumor being killed.

Norman Cousins's approach to his own serious illness (one of the earliest of the "alternative" therapies) involved a clear-cut change of context. He took himself out of the hospital and into a hotel, where he exchanged intravenous tubes and sterile conditions for old Marx Brothers films. In *Anatomy of an Illness*, he describes the shift that took place in his mind as swift and complete.[29]

There are many other alternative healing methods than those described here. The point is simply to show the similarity between these methods and the definitions of mindfulness described earlier. Whenever we try to heal ourselves, and not abdicate this responsibility completely to doctors, each step is mindful. For example, we question destructive categories of disease (such as the image of cancer as a death sentence). We welcome new information, whether from our bodies or from books. We look at our illness from more than a single perspective (the medical one). We work on changing contexts, whether it is a stressful workplace or a depressing rather than a positive view of the hospital. Finally, the attempt to stay healthy rather than to be "made well" necessarily involves us with process rather than outcome.

In applying mindfulness theory to health, I have so far worked mostly with elderly people. Success in increasing longevity by making more cognitive demands on nursing home residents (as mentioned earlier) or by teaching meditation or techniques of flexible, novel thinking gives us strong reason to believe that the same techniques could be used to improve health and shorten illness earlier in life.[30] In one recent experiment we gave arthritis sufferers various interesting word problems to increase their mental activity. For example, subjects in this group were given slightly doctored sayings such as "a bird in the bush is worth two in the hand," and were asked to explain them. Comparison subjects were given the old familiar versions. In the mindful group, not only did subjective measures of comfort and enjoyment change, but some of the chemistry of the disease (sedimentation rates of the blood in this case) was affected as well.[31] There were no significant changes in the comparison group.

In this chapter I've implicitly described two ways in which we have learned to influence health: exchanging unhealthy mindsets for healthy ones and increasing a generally mindful state. The latter is more lasting and results in more personal control. The real value of "active placebos" will come when people put them to work for themselves. Consider how you learned to ride a bike. Someone older and taller held on to the seat to keep you from falling, until you found your balance. Then, without your knowledge, that strong hand let go and you were on your own. You controlled the bicycle even without knowing it. The same is true for all of us most of our lives. We control our health, or the course of our diseases, without really knowing that we do. On the bike, however, at some point you realized that you were in control. Now may be the time to learn how to recognize and use our control over illness.

In a sense, we should be able to "take" a placebo instead of a pill. Conceiving of the mind and body as one means that wherever we put the mind, we may be able to put our bodies. For most of us, at present at least, the mind may have to be fooled to reach a healthy place. Once we learn how to put it there consciously, the evidence suggests that the body may well follow. In a book aptly called *New Bottles for New Wine*, Julian Huxley quotes his grandfather, the great nineteenth-century scientist Thomas Huxley, on the subject of belief: "Everyone should be able to give a reason for the faith that is in him. My faith is in human possibilities."[32]

EPILOGUE

*

Beyond Mindfulness

Corin: And how like you this shepherd's life, Master Touchstone?
Touchstone: Truly, shepherd, in respect of itself, it is a good life; but in respect that it is a shepherd's life, it is naught. In respect that it is solitary, I like it very well; but in respect that it is private, it is a very vile life. Now in respect it is in the fields, it pleaseth me well; but in respect it is not in the court, it is tedious. As it is a spare life, look you, it fits my humour well; but as there is no more plenty in it, it goes much against my stomach. Hast any philosophy in thee shepherd?
WILLIAM SHAKESPEARE
As You Like It, act 3, scene 2

*

Whenever I give a talk about mindfulness, I'm inevitably asked certain questions: How can people possibly be mindful all the time? Doesn't it take too much effort?

If we keep making mindful new distinctions, how would we ever make a decision?

When examples of mindfulness such as those in the second half of this book do not seem to answer the questions, I try various metaphors. For instance, to understand why it is not necessary to be mindful about everything all of the time, think of the brain as a large corporation, with a Chief Executive Officer. This CEO is charged with monitoring the overall functioning of the corporation and its transactions with the outside world—but does not, cannot, and should not actively monitor everything. The job of maintaining the heating system at corporate headquarters, for example, is routinely delegated to the custodial staff. The CEO need not attend to it unless and until it requires a major investment for replacement. Similarly most of us can routinely delegate the responsibility for our breathing. We need not become "mindful" of it until a cold, a passionate kiss, or preparation for a marathon makes breathing a problem. Many complex activities, such as driving a car, require keen attention in the early learning stages but don't require mindfulness later on. The effective person—like the effective CEO—allocates attention wisely, choosing where and when to be mindful.

The effective CEO must also be mindful about his or her own job. In a crisis, the CEO who mindlessly applies routine solutions learned in an MBA program or used on previous occasions may fail to meet the challenge. A mindful CEO can be mindful on two levels: by simply resolving the crisis in a mindful manner, or by using it as an opportunity for innovation.

For example, when employee productivity declines, the mindful CEO would notice and might increase management supervision over the workers while a mindfully mindful CEO might rethink the whole employment situation and consider stock option plans or a corporate day-care center.

This second-order mindfulness, choosing what to be mindful about, is something that we can be doing all the time. Though we cannot and would not want to be mindful of everything simultaneously, we can always be mindful of something. The most important function task for any CEO, and for the rest of us, is choosing what to be mindful about. Rather than spending all day inspecting every expense account or widget in the factory, the mindfully mindful executive chooses where to pay attention.

And yet, I'm also asked, isn't it necessary to be mindless about some things in order to come to a decision? Take the choice of a restaurant: Should I go to a Chinese or a French restaurant for dinner? If I decide on Chinese food, should I go to Joyce Lee's, Peking Delight, Lucky Eden, or Ming's Hunan? Joyce Lee's has the best mooshi chicken but Peking Delight has better spare ribs—sometimes. Lucky Eden is more convenient, but Ming's has more privacy. Peking Delight is less expensive. If I go to Joyce Lee's, maybe I'll run into Norm, Carol, Carrie, and Andrea there—it would be nice to see them tonight. But what about that new Thai restaurant that just opened down the block?

The problem here is not the need to survey all the

alternatives mindfully; the problem is the belief that if you construct more and more arguments and ask yourself even more questions, then you will eventually know *the* answer. Typically, we believe that there are purely rational ways to make choices and that if we can't come to a decision it is because there are insufficient data. Second-order mindfulness recognizes that there is no right answer. Decision making is independent of data gathering. Data don't make decisions, people do—either with ease or with difficulty. Ambivalence about a decision, or about an individual—friend, lover, spouse—becomes a problem if we are convinced that more information can resolve the ambivalence in one direction or another. Generating more questions will not help because there is no logical stopping point. We might just as well pick a moment to stop asking questions, recognize that it is an arbitrary moment, and then make a "gut" decision. We can then work on making the decision right rather than obsess about making the right decision.

To understand this presumed pitfall of mindfulness, and ways around it, we can look at more serious examples. Take the case of a physician or judge interested in the question of whether to prolong life in the face of intolerable pain. Tom Schelling, a colleague in the John F. Kennedy School of Government at Harvard, suggested that providing a person, for example, someone suffering from a wretched disease, with the means to bring about his or her own death might have two quite different consequences. On the one hand, shorter lives may result if people take swift advantage of this opportunity. On the other hand, the increase in control over one's own destiny might lead people to want to live longer than they would without such control.[1]

The conflicting information brought by these mindful reflections might seem to make the decision more difficult. It actually throws the discussion back to where it belongs: on individual values. The doctor, judge, and patient must decide between the principle of prolonging life at all costs and the "right" to determine the quality of life. Making more distinctions will not result in absolute right answers.

Living in a mindful state may be likened to living in a transparent house. In the houses in which most of us now live, if we were in the living room and needed an object (idea) that was in the basement, we might not be aware of its presence. But in our transparent house, objects would be ever available. When in the living room, we could still see the object in the basement even if we chose not to think about it or use it at the moment. If we were taught mindfully, conditionally, we could be in this ever-ready state of mind. Thus, while it is true that we cannot think of everything at once, everything can be kept available. To be alert in this fashion, open to new perspectives and new information, is not effortful. What may take effort is the switch from a mindless to a mindful mode, just as in physics effort is required to change the course of a moving body and energy is required to put a still body into motion.

Mindful awareness of different options gives us

greater control. This feeling of greater control, in turn, encourages us to be more mindful. Rather than being a chore, mindfulness engages us in a continuing momentum.

One reason mindfulness may seem effortful is because of the pain of negative thoughts. When thoughts are uncomfortable, people often struggle to erase them. The pain, however, does not come from mindful awareness of these thoughts, but from a single-minded understanding of the painful event. A mindful new perspective would erase the pain more effectively.

Anxious thinking has similarly given mindfulness a bad name. Imagine you are in a car that makes an ominous grinding noise. Surely, you say, mindfully considering all the things that could be wrong is not something we would want to do. However, being mindlessly certain that the noise has an alarming cause is neither pleasant nor helpful. At the least, if there is a solution, the more mindful person is more likely to find it. Anxiety is not mindful, and mindlessness is not relaxing. Indeed, stressful events are probably less stressful when considered from multiple perspectives.

While some people think that mindfulness takes a lot of work, the research discussed in this book shows that mindfulness leads to feelings of control, greater freedom of action, and less burnout.

Even with the best definitions, the finest research designs, and the most careful answers to each question, mindfulness, like the brook we compared it to earlier, cannot be captured, cannot be analyzed once and for all. The experiments my colleagues and I have done, and the anecdotes from ordinary life told in this book, only hint at the enormous potential of the mindful state. In trying to quantify it, or reduce it to a formula, we risk losing sight of the whole. C. M. Gillmore tells a splendid fable, a cautionary tale for those who insist on tidy, definitive results:

Once upon a time, a highly respected and revered psychometrician of a great university was sailing about from sea to sea enjoying a well-deserved vacation. On a fine sunny day, his ship put in at a very small harbor of a very small atoll where, the crew informed him, they occasionally stopped to leave food for three hermits who were the only inhabitants. Sure enough, there they were standing on the sand to greet the Professor, their long white beards and their white lab coats blowing in the breeze, looking exactly as hermits should look, and their delight in seeing him was gratifying. For, they explained, they had come out to this solitary archipelago long, long ago, in order to enter into pure animal behavior research, and not be interrupted by the cares of the world, such as teaching, faculty meetings, and the myriad of other distractions. But, during these many years, they had forgotten a good deal of the proper statistical methods taught them at the University and were most eager to refresh themselves at the fount of the professor's wisdom.

So the wise doctor spoke with them for many hours, reviving their memories of simple and complex designs, of methods and techniques necessary for publications, and instructed them so they could recognize the proper statistical test for their data once more. Feeling that he had done a fine day's work, the psychometrician returned to his ship and sailed away.

At dawn—for he was ever an early riser—he was sitting in his deck chair in the clear light and against the bright horizon he saw a strange—an unbelievable—sight. After trying for some time to identify a boat, or a canoe, or a kayak, or even a raft, the Professor sent for the captain, and they stared through the binoculars and soon had to admit the impossible, for a rhesus monkey was riding on the back of a large porpoise. So there seemed nothing to do but lean over the rail as the monkey and fish guided to below it. The monkey cried out,

"Dear and wise Professor, we have been trained in the laboratory of the hermits, and they crave your forgiveness for sending us to trouble you with their difficulty, but none of them can remember how you said to determine the denominator degrees of freedom, and since they must know this in order to get their results published . . ."[2]

In the laboratory of the hermits, no one noticed that the monkeys could talk.

*

Notes

Chapter 1

1. E. Langer and J. Rodin, "The Effects of Enhanced Personal Responsibility for the Aged: A Field Experiment in an Institutional Setting," *Journal of Personality and Social Psychology* 34 (1976): 191–198; J. Rodin and E. Langer, "Long-term Effects of a Control-Relevant Intervention Among the Institutionalized Aged," *Journal of Personality and Social Psychology* 35 (1977): 897–902.

2. C. Gersick and J. R. Hackman, "Habitual Routines in Task-Performing Groups," *Organizational Behavior and Human Decision Processes*, in press.

3. I. Illich, *Medical Nemesis* (New York: Pantheon, 1976).

Chapter 2

1. C. Trungpa, *Cutting Through Spiritual Materialism* (Boulder and London: Shambhala, 1973).

2. T'ai P'ing, *Kuang Chi* [Extensive Records Made in the Period of Peace and Prosperity] (978 A.D.), as cited in

Jorge Luis Borges, *Libro de Los Seres Imaginarios* (Buenos Aires: Editorial Kiersa S.A., Fauna China, 1967), p. 88.

3. L. Solomons and G. Stein, "Normal Motor Automation," *Psychological Review* 36 (1896): 492–572.

4. E. Langer, A. Blank, and B. Chanowitz, "The Mindlessness of Ostensibly Thoughtful Action: The Role of Placebic Information in Interpersonal Interaction, *Journal of Personality and Social Psychology* 36 (1978): 635–642.

5. Ibid.

6. To understand the more complex relationship between automatic information processing and mindlessness, compare E. Langer, "Minding Matters," in L. Berkowitz, ed., *Advances in Experimental Social Psychology* (New York: Academic Press, in press) and W. Schneider and R. M. Schiffrin, "Controlled and Automatic Human Information Processing: I. Detection, Search, and Attention," *Psychological Review* 84 (1977): 1–66.

7. The correct answer is 8. A similar quiz was printed on the business card of the Copy Service of Miami, Inc.

Chapter 3

1. E. Langer and C. Weinman, "When Thinking Disrupts Intellectual Performance: Mindlessness on an Overlearned Task," *Personality and Social Psychology Bulletin* 7 (1981): 240–243.

2. G. A. Kimble and L. Perlmuter, "The Problem of Volition," *Psychological Review* 77 (1970): 212–218.

3. B. Chanowitz and E. Langer, "Premature Cognitive

Commitment," *Journal of Personality and Social Psychology* 41 (1981): 1051–1063.

4. The study actually employed a 2 x 2 factorial design in which the variables of interest were relevance (i.e., likelihood of having the disorder, 10% vs. 80%) and instructions to think about the problem (yes vs. no).

5. S. Freud (1912), "A Note on the Unconscious in Psychoanalysis," in *The Standard Edition of the Complete Psychological Works of Sigmund Freud*, ed. J. Strachey, vol. 12 (London: Hogarth Press, 1959), p. 265.

6. Plato, *Republic,* Book IX (Oxford: Clarendon Press, 1888), p. 281, as cited in M. Erdelyi, *Psychoanalysis* (New York: Freeman, 1985).

7. Scientists know that while one can fail to find evidence *for* a hypothesis—the hypothesis in this case being that some particular ability is unlimited—that is not the same thing as finding evidence *against* a hypothesis. One cannot prove that there are no limits. One may just keep surpassing past limits.

8. D. Dewsbury, "Effects of Novelty on Copulatory Behavior. The Coolidge Effect and Related Phenomenon," *Psychological Bulletin* 89 (1981): 464–482.

9. J. E. Orme, *Time, Experience and Behavior* (London: Illif Books, 1969).

10. E. Mach, *Science of Mechanics* (Chicago: Open Court Publishing, 1983).

11. R. Arnis and B. Frost, "Human Visual Ecology and Orientation Anestropies in Acuity," *Science* 182 (1973): 729–731.

12. D. Holmes and B. K. Houston, "Effectiveness of Situation Redefinition and Affective Isolation in Coping

with Stress," *Journal of Personality and Social Psychology* 29 (1974): 212–218.

13. *The Boston Globe*, March 11, 1980.

14. D. Brown, "Stimulus-Similarity and the Anchoring of Subjective Scales," *American Journal of Psychology* 66 (1953): 199–214.

15. L. Postman, J. Bruner, and E. McGinnies, "Personal Values as Selective Factors in Perception," *Journal of Abnormal Psychology* 48 (1948): 142–154.

16. Allport-Vernon Study of Values (Boston: Houghton Mifflin, 1931.)

Chapter 4

1. T. Levitt, "Marketing Myopia," *Harvard Business Review* 38, no. 4 (1960): 45–56, reprinted in 53, no. 5 (1975): 26–174.

2. E. Langer, J. Johnson, and H. Botwinick, "Nothing Succeeds Like Success, Except . . . ," in E. Langer, *The Psychology of Control* (Los Angeles: Sage Pùblications, 1983).

3. E. Langer and A. Benevento, "Self-Induced Dependence," *Journal of Personality and Social Psychology* 36 (1978): 886–893.

4. S. Milgram, *Obedience to Authority* (New York: Harper & Row, 1974).

5. E. Langer and H. Newman, "Post-divorce Adaptation and the Attribution of Responsibility," *Sex Roles* 7 (1981): 223–232.

6. E. Langer, L. Perlmuter, B. Chanowitz, and R. Rubin,

"Two New Applications of Mindlessness Theory: Alcoholism and Aging," *Journal of Aging Studies*, Vol. 2:3 (1988) 289–299.

7. A. Luchins and E. Luchins, "Mechanization in Problem-Solving: The Effect of Einstellung," *Psychological Monographs* 54, no. 6 (1942).

8. M. Seligman, *Helplessness: On Depression, Development and Death* (San Francisco: Freeman, 1975).

9. C. P. Richter, "The Phenomenon of Sudden Death in Animals and Man," *Psychosomatic Medicine* 19 (1957): 191–198.

10. H. Lefcourt, as cited in Seligman, *Helplessness*.

11. W. James, "The World We Live In," *The Philosophy of William James* (New York: Modern Library, 1953).

12. Langer, Perlmuter, Chanowitz, and Rubin, "Two New Applications of Mindlessness Theory."

13. Happiness is not stereotypically related to age in the same way that lack of alertness and independence are. Accordingly, participants did not evaluate themselves as happier people, nor did independent raters do so. This indicates that the ratings were not indiscriminate.

14. C. Dickens, *Great Expectations* (1860–1861). (Cambridge, MA: Riverside Press, 1877), p. 51.

Chapter 5

1. L. Tolstoy, *War and Peace*, 1869 trans. Louise and Aylmer Maude (Oxford: Oxford University Press, 1983).

2. J. Bruner, J. Goodnow, and G. Austin, *A Study of Think-*

ing (New York: Wiley, 1956); R. Brown, *Words and Things* (New York: Free Press, 1958).

3. S. Freud (1907). "Creative Writers and Daydreaming," in *The Standard Edition of the Complete Psychological Works of Sigmund Freud*, ed. J. Strachey, vol. 9 (London: Hogarth Press, 1959), 143–144.

4. E. Langer and C. Weinman, "Mindlessness, Confidence and Accuracy" (1976), as described in B. Chanowitz and E. Langer, "Knowing More (or Less) Than You Can Show: Understanding Control Through the Mind-lessness/Mindfulness Distinction," in *Human Helplessness*, ed. M. E. P. Seligman and J. Garber. (New York: Academic Press, 1980).

5. E. Jones and R. Nisbett, "The Actor and the Observer: Divergent Perceptions of the Causes of Behavior," in *Attributions: Perceiving the Causes of Behavior*, ed. E. Jones et al. (Morristown, NJ: General Learning Press, 1972).

6. I. Lindahl, "Chernobyl: The Geopolitical Dimensions," *American Scandinavian Review* 75, no. 3 (1987): 29–40.

7. These points of view are different in another way that is important in the study of psychology. The more specific the level of analysis, the greater the likelihood of unpredictability. The study of personality does not generally pay attention to the individual's prototypical level of analysis. As in the example cited, differences on this dimension, whether stemming from trait or even state, may give rise to interpersonal difficulty.

8. If one makes a *conscious decision* to consider alternative frames for complex negative information in this way, one cannot sensibly be accused of "rationalizing."

9. E. Langer and L. Thompson, "Mindlessness and Self-

Esteem: The Observer's Perspective," Harvard University (1987).

10. E. Langer, I. Janis, and J. Wolfer, "Reduction of Psychological Stress in Surgical Patients," *Journal of Experimental Social Psychology* 11 (1975): 155–165.

11. R. Pascale and N. Athos, *The Art of Japanese Management* (New York: Simon & Schuster, 1981).

12. S. Druker, "Unified Field Based Ethics: Vedic Psychology's Description of the Highest Stage of Moral Reasoning," *Modern Science and Vedic Science*, in press.

13. See E. Langer, *Minding Matters* (chapter 2, note 6) for a discussion of the latent vs. expressed modes of mindfulness. Only the expressed mode is being considered in this book.

14. A. Deikman, "De-automatization and the Mystic Experience," *Psychiatry* 29 (1966): 329–343.

Chapter 6

1. E. Langer and J. Rodin, "The Effects of Enhanced Personal Responsibility for the Aged: A Field Experiment in an Institutional Setting," *Journal of Personality and Social Psychology* 34 (1976): 191–198; J. Rodin and E. Langer, "Long-Term Effects of a Control-Relevant Intervention Among the Institutionalized Aged," *Journal of Personality and Social Psychology* 35 (1977): 275–282.

2. E. Langer and L. Perlmuter, "Behavioral Monitoring as a Technique to Influence Depression and Self-Knowledge for Elderly Adults," Harvard University. (1988).

3. L. Perlmuter and E. Langer, "The Effects of Behavioral

Monitoring on the Perception of Control," *The Clinical Gerontologist* 1 (1979): 37–43.

4. M. M. Baltes and E. M. Barton, "Behavioral Analysis of Aging: A Review of the Operant Model and Research," *International Journal of Behavior Development* 2 (1979): 297–320.

5. J. Avorn and E. Langer, "Induced Disability in Nursing Home Patients: A Controlled Trial," *Journal of American Geriatric Society* 30 (1982): 397–400; E. Langer and J. Avorn, "The Psychosocial Environment of the Elderly: Some Behavioral and Health Implications," in *Congregate Housing for Older People*, ed. J. Seagle and R. Chellis (Lexington, MA: Lexington Books, 1981).

6. E. Langer, J. Rodin, P. Beck, C. Weinman, and L. Spitzer, "Environmental Determinants of Memory Improvement in Late Adulthood," *Journal of Personality and Social Psychology* 37 (1979): 2003–2013.

7. E. Langer, P. Beck, R. Janoff-Bulman and C. Timko, "The Relationship Between Cognitive Deprivation and Longevity in Senile and Nonsenile Elderly Populations," *Academic Psychology Bulletin* 6 (1984): 211–226.

8. S. de Beauvoir, *Old Age* (London: Andre Deutsch Ltd., 1972).

9. Cicero, *Two Essays on Old Age and Friendship*, trans. E. S. Shuckburg (London: Macmillan & Co., 1900).

10. J. Rowe and R. Kahn, "Human Aging: Usual and Successful," *Science* 273 (1987): 143–149.

11. F. Scott-Maxwell, *The Measure of My Days* (New York: Knopf, 1972).

12. A. Mulvey and E. Langer, as discussed in J. Rodin and E. Langer, "Aging Labels: The Decline of Control and

the Fall of Self-Esteem," *Journal of Social Issues* 36 (1980): 12–29.

13. P. Katzman and T. Carasu (1975). "Differential Diagnosis of Dementia," in *Neurological and Sensory Disorders in the Elderly*, ed. W. S. Fields (Miami, FL: Symposia Specialist Medical Books), 103–104.

14. G. Kolata, "New Neurons Form in Adulthood," *Science* 224 (1984): 1325–1326.

15. B. A. Fiala, J. N. Joyce, and W. T. Greenough, "Environmental Complexity Modulates Growth of Granule Cell Dendrites in Developing but not Adult Hippocampus of Rats," *Experimental Neurology* 59 (1978): 372–383; W. Greenough and F. Volkmar, "Patterns of Dendritic Branching in Occipital Cortex of Rats Reared in Complex Environments," *Experimental Neurology* 40 (1973): 491–508; D. Krech, M. R. Rosenzweig, and E. L. Bennet, "Relations Between Brain Chemistry and Problem Solving Among Rats Raised in Enriched and Impoverished Environments," *Journal of Comparative and Physiological Psychology* 55 (1962): 801–807; F. Volkmar and W. Greenough, "Rearing Complexity Affects Branching of Dendrites in the Visual Cortex of the Rat," *Science* 176 (1972): 1445–1447; R. A. Cummins and R. N. Walsh, "Synaptic Changes in Differentially Reared Mice," *Australian Psychologist* 2, no. 229 (1976).

16. M. Rosenzweig, E. L. Bennett, and M. Diamond, "Brain Changes in Response to Experience," *Scientific American* 226, no. 2 (1972): 22–29.

17. L. Strachey, *Queen Victoria* (New York and London: Harcourt Brace Jovanovich, 1921).

18. W. James, *Letters of William James*, Vol. 1, ed. H. James (Boston: Atlantic Monthly Press, 1920).

19. E. Langer, B. Chanowitz, M. Palmerino, S. Jacobs, M. Rhodes, and P. Thayer (1988). "Nonsequential Development and Aging," in *Higher Stages of Human Development: Perspectives on Adult Growth*, ed. C. Alexander and E. Langer (New York: Oxford University Press, in press).

20. We contacted twenty of the country's leading research physicians who have specialties in geriatric medicine, heart disease, and endocrinology. Each pointed out that there do not seem to be any reliable measures of aging. "If we put a fifty-year-old in one room and a seventy-year-old in another," we asked, "how would you tell them apart?" Virtually each physician said, "It would be extremely difficult. The best guess would be outward appearance. The only possible exception would be X rays of the skeleton. The age-related changes of osteoarthritis, particularly on the spine, are quite distinctive. . . . However these changes are in no way uniform with age and sometimes begin to develop quite early in middle age and sometimes not until very advanced age." Another physician said, "One needs baseline measures for each individual." One of the most sophisticated researchers in the area said, "In studies of the variables that change most dramatically with age (cardiac function, pulmonary function, renal function) there are always old individuals (over eighty) who perform as well as the average thirty-year-old, and there are usually young individuals who perform at the same level as the average old individual." This lack of agreed-upon measures made it rather difficult to design our study. We settled on measures of body function that are at least somewhat correlated with aging. There are common changes in appearance that occur during old age. The nose elongates, the eyes seem to dull and become lusterless and often watery. The skin becomes wrinkled and dry, and

dark spots, moles, or warts may appear. The hair turns gray or white or is lost. The shoulders droop. The upper arms become flabby and the lower arms smaller. The hands become thin and the veins become quite visible. In the same way, visual acuity decreases and people tend to become more farsighted. The ability to hear high tones diminishes and taste buds atrophy. On the psychological side are decrements in the capacity to learn and remember newly learned information. Gait slows, as does reaction time. With these in mind we developed a battery of measures to assess improvements in the domain of physical and psychological competence as a function of our "treatment."

21. R. Bales and S. Cohen, *SYMLOG: A System for Multiple Level Observation of Groups* (New York: Free Press, 1979).

22. E. Langer and J. Rodin, "Effects of Enhanced Personal Responsibility for the Aged"; J. Rodin and E. Langer, "Long-Term Effects of Control-Relevant Intervention."

23. Limited funds precluded a follow-up investigation. One might expect a return to lower levels of competence, however, with a return to living in low-expectation contexts.

Chapter 7

1. H. Poincaré, "Intuition and Logic Mathematics," *Mathematics Teacher* 62, no. 3 (1969): 205-212.

2. I. Duncan, as quoted in G. Bateson, *Steps to an Ecology of Mind* (San Francisco: Chandler Publications, 1972), p. 137.

3. As quoted in P. Goldberg, *The Intuitive Edge* (Los Angeles: J.P. Tarcher, 1983).

4. W. Churchill, as cited in P. Goldberg, *The Intuitive Edge* (Los Angeles: J.P. Tarcher, 1983).

5. J. Bruner and B. Clinchy, "Towards a Disciplined Intuition, in *Learning about Learning*, no. 15, ed. J. Bruner (Bureau of Research Co-operative Research Monograph).

6. E. Langer and A. Piper, "The Prevention of Mindlessness," *Journal of Personality and Social Psychology* 53 (1987): 280-287.

7. E. Langer, A. Piper, and J. Friedus, "Preventing Mindlessness: A Positive Side of Dyslexia," Harvard University (1986).

8. T. Amabile, *The Social Psychology of Creativity* (New York: Springer-Verlag, 1983).

9. J. W. Getzels and P. Jackson, "Family Environment and Cognitive Style: A Study of the Sources of Highly Intelligent and Highly Creative Adolescents," *American Sociological Review* 26: 351-359.

10. E. Langer and J. Joss, as described in E. Langer, M. Hatem, J. Joss, and M. Howell, "The Mindful Consequences of Teaching Uncertainty for Elementary School and College Students," *Creativity Research Journal*, in press.

11. Further confirmation of the value of conditional learning can be found in G. Salomon and T. Globerson, "Skill May Not Be Enough: The Role of Mindfulness in Learning and Transfer," *International Journal of Educational Research* (1987) 11:623–627, and G. Solomon and D. Perkins, "Rocky Roads to Transfer: Rethinking

Mechanisms of a Neglected Phenomenon," *Educational Researcher*, in press (April 1989).

12. S. J. Gould, "The Case of the Creeping Fox Terrier Clone," *Natural History* 97, no. 1: 16-24.

13. J. Barchillon, "Creativity and Its Inhibition in Child Prodigies," in *Personality Dimensions of Creativity* (New York: Lincoln Institute for Psychotherapy, 1961).

14. J. P. Guilford, *The Nature of Human Intelligence* (New York: McGraw-Hill, 1967).

15. The more educated one is, the harder it may be to find absolute right answers. Lions in a group are called a *pride* of lions, making *herd* an appropriate answer. A comparison of an animal to an emotion would make *vanity* appropriate. The "correct" answer on a test may be unclear if it is written as if it were context-free. The most mindful mind, free of context, can see much more than is intended.

16. Watching television is another pursuit in which the use of novel perspectives may be beneficial. Even television may be watched mindfully. In a study conducted with Alison Piper, I had subjects watch "Dynasty" from different perspectives. The results—which are described in E. Langer and A. Piper, "Television from a Mindful/ Mindless Perspective," *Applied Social Psychology Annual*, Vol. 8, Los Angeles: Sage Publications, 1988—included increased control for the viewer and other positive consequences.

17. J. Piaget, "Psychology and Epistemology" (New York: Grossman, 1971), p. vii, quoted in G. Holton, *The Advancement of Science, and Its Burdens* (Cambridge: Cambridge University Press, 1986).

Chapter 8

1. T. Levitt, "Marketing Myopia," *The Harvard Business Review* 38, no. 4 (1960): 45–56, reprinted in 53, no. 5 (1975): 26–174.

2. A. Karsten (1928), "Mental Satiation," in *Field Theory as Human Science*, ed. J. de Rivera (New York: Gardner Press, 1976).

3. J. R. Kelly and J. E. McGrath, "Effects of Time Limits of Task Types on Task Performance and Interaction of Four-Person Groups," *Journal of Personality and Social Psychology* 49 (1985): 395–407.

4. Rosabeth Moss Kanter and Howard Stevenson, both of Harvard Business School, write about a version of this idea in business: R. Kanter, *The Change Masters: Innovation for Productivity in the American Corporation* (New York: Simon & Schuster, 1983); H. Stevenson and W. Sahlman, "How Small Companies Should Handle Advisers," *Harvard Business Review* 88, no. 2 (1988): 28–34. Also, Irving Janis describes a version of this idea in the political arena: I. Janis, *Victims of Groupthink* (Boston: Houghton Mifflin, 1972).

5. R. Fisher and W. Urey, *Getting to Yes* (Boston: Houghton Mifflin, 1981).

6. T. Levitt, "Marketing Myopia."

7. E. Langer and D. Heffernan, "Mindful Managing: Confident but Uncertain Managers," Harvard University. (1988).

8. E. Langer and J. Sviokla, "Charisma from a Mindfulness Perspective," Harvard University. (1988).

9. E. Langer, D. Heffernan, and M. Kiester, "Reducing

Burnout in an Institutional Setting: An Experimental Investigation," Harvard University. (1988).

10. M. P. Follet, *Dynamic Administration: The Collected Papers of Mary Parker Follett* (Bath, England: Bath Management, 1941), quoted in P. Graham, *Dynamic Management: The Follett Way* (London: Professional Publishing, 1987).

Chapter 9

1. R. Brown, *Words and Things* (New York: The Free Press, 1956); J. Bruner, "Personality Dynamics and the Process of Perceiving," in *Perception: An Approach to Personality*, ed. R. R. Blake and G. V. Ramsey (New York: Ronald Press, 1951), pp. 121–147.

2. E. Langer, and R. Abelson, "A Patient by Any Other Name . . . : Clinician Group Differences in Labelling Bias," *Journal of Consulting and Clinical Psychology* 42 (1974): 4–9.

3. J. Swift (1726), *Gulliver's Travels* (New York: Dell, 1961).

4. E. Langer and L. Imber, "The Role of Mindlessness in the Perception of Deviance," *Journal of Personality and Social Psychology* 39 (1980): 360–367.

5. E. Langer, S. Taylor, S. Fiske, and B. Chanowitz, "Stigma, Staring and Discomfort: A Novel Stimulus Hypothesis," *Journal of Experimental Social Psychology* 12 (1976): 451–463.

6. A. Piper, E. Langer, and J. Friedus, "Preventing Mindlessness: A Positive Side of Dyslexia," Harvard University (1987).

7. H. Madjid, "The Handicapped Person as a Scientific Puzzle in Search of a Solution," Paper presented at the annual meeting of the American Academy for the Advancement of Science, Boston, 1988.

8. E. E. Jones and S. Berglas, "Control of Attributions About the Self Through Self-Handicapping Strategies: The Appeal of Alcohol and the Role of Underachievement," *Personality and Social Psychology Bulletin* 4 (1978): 200–206.

9. E. Langer and B. Chanowitz, "A New Perspective for the Study of Disability," in *Attitudes Towards Persons with Disabilities*, ed. H. E. Yuker (New York: Springer Press, 1987). The best solution, however, might be to have high expectations and, as seen in Chapter 5, see failures simply as ineffective solutions rather than indications of lack of self-worth.

10. D. McClelland, *The Achieving Society* (New York: The Free Press, 1961).

11. E. Langer, R. Bashner, and B. Chanowitz, "Decreasing Prejudice by Increasing Discrimination," *Journal of Personality and Social Psychology* 49 (1985): 113–120. The study, simplified here, actually used a 2 × 2 factorial design in which the variables of interest were mindfulness training (high versus low) × target person (disabled versus nondisabled). The advanced student of psychology is encouraged to read the original work for more subtle details.

Chapter 10

1. Sir Charles Sherrington, *Man on His Nature*, 2nd ed. (New York: Doubleday Anchor Books, 1953), p. 194.

2. R. Katz, *Boiling Energy* (Cambridge, MA: Harvard University Press, 1982).

3. A. Eddington, *The Nature of the Physical World* (Ann Arbor, MI: University of Michigan Press, 1958).

4. S. Schacter and J. Singer, "Cognitive, Social, and Physiological Determinants of Emotional State," *Psychological Review* 69 (1962): 379–399.

5. W. James, "What Is Emotion?" *Mind* 9 (1883): 188–204.

6. C. Lange, *The Emotions* (Baltimore: Williams & Wilkens, 1922); W. Cannon, "The James Lange Theory of Emotion: A Critical Examination and Alternative Theory," *American Journal of Psychology* 39 (1927): 106–124.

7. R. Zajonc, "Attitudinal Effects of Mere Exposure," *Journal of Personality and Social Psychology Monograph Supplement* 9 (no. 2, part 2) (1968): 1–27.

8. P. Brickman, *Commitment, Conflict and Caring* (Englewood Cliffs, NJ: Prentice-Hall, 1987).

9. W. James (1890), *The Principles of Psychology* (Cambridge, MA: Harvard University Press, 1981).

10. H. K. Beecher, "Relationship of Significance of Wound to Pain Experience," *Journal of American Medical Association* 161 (1956): 1609–1613.

11. R. S. Ulrich, "View from a Window May Influence Recovery from Surgery," *Science* 224 (1984): 420–421.

12. Awareness of the fact that novelty/familiarity is a social construction makes possible a good deal of personal control. For example, to decrease anxiety one can look for the familiar elements in a situation while, if one is bored, searching out novel features would be an advantageous strategy.

13. K. Järvinen, "Can Ward Rounds Be a Danger to Patients with Myocardial Infarction?" *British Medical Journal* 1 (4909) (1955): 318–320.

14. E. Langer, M. Dillon, R. Kurtz, and M. Katz, "Believing is Seeing," Harvard University (1988).

15. R. W. Bell, C. E. Miller, J. M. Ordy, and C. Rolsten, "Effects of Population Density and Living Space Upon Neuroanatomy, Neurochemistry and Behavior in the C57B1-10 Mouse," *Journal of Comparative and Physiological Psychology* 75 (1971): 258–263.

16. M. Rosenzweig, E. L. Bennett, and M. Diamond, "Brain Changes in Response to Experience," *Scientific American* 226, no. 2 (1972): 22–29.

17. R. Totman, *Social Causes of Illness* (New York: Pantheon Books, 1979), p. 96.

18. G. A. Marlatt and D. J. Rohsenow, "Cognitive Processes in Alcohol Use: Expectancy and the Balanced Placebo Design," in *Advances in Substance Abuse: Behavioral and Biological Research,* Vol. 1, ed. N. K. Mello (1980), p. 199.

19. G. Wilson and D. Abrams, "Effects of Alcohol on Social Anxiety and Physiological Arousal: Cognitive versus Pharmacological Procedures," *Cognitive Therapy and Research* 1 (1977): 195–210.

20. L. Robbins, D. David, and D. Nurco, "How Permanent was Vietnam Drug Addiction?" *American Journal of Public Health* 64 (1974): 38–43.

21. S. Siegel, R. Hirsan, M. Krank, and Y. McGully, "Heroin Overdose Death: Contribution of Drugs as Actual Environmental Cues," *Science* 216 (1982): 436–437.

22. J. Margolis and E. Langer, "An Analysis of Addiction from a Mindlessness/Mindfulness Perspective," *Psychology of Addictive Behavior*, in press.

23. Ibid.

24. R. Ader and C. Cohen, "Behaviorally Conditioned Immunosuppression and Nurive Systemic Lupus Eurythemastosus," *Science* 215 (1982): 1534–1536.

25. S. F. Kelly and R. J. Kelly, *Hypnosis* (Reading, MA: Addison-Wesley, 1985), p. 21.

26. L. Thomas, *The Medusa and the Snail* (New York: Harper & Row, 1957).

27. A. H. C. Sinclair-Gieben and D. Chalmers, "Evaluation of Treatment of Warts by Hypnosis," *Lancet* (October 3, 1959): 480–482.

28. O. C. Simonton, S. Matthews-Simonton, and J. L. Creighton, *Getting Well Again* (Los Angeles: J. P. Tarcher, 1978).

29. N. Cousins, *Anatomy of an Illness as Perceived by the Patient* (New York: W. W. Norton, 1979).

30. E. Langer, J. Rodin, P. Beck, C. Weinman, and L. Spitzer, "Environmental Determinants of Memory Improvement in Late Adulthood," *Journal of Personality and Social Psychology* 37 (1979): 2003–2013; E. Langer, P. Beck, R. Janoff-Bulman, and C. Timko, "The Relationship Between Cognitive Deprivation and Longevity in Senile and Nonsenile Elderly Populations," *Academic Psychology Bulletin* 6 (1984): 211–226; C. Alexander, E. Langer, R. Newman, H. Chandler, and J. Davies, "Transcendental Meditation, Mindfulness and Longevity: An Experimental Study with the Elderly," *Journal of Personality and Social Psychology* 57, no. 6 (1989): 950–964.

31. E. Langer, S. Field, W. Paches, and E. Abrams, "A Mindful Treatment for Arthritis," Harvard University (1988).

32. Thomas Huxley, as quoted in J. Huxley, *New Bottles for New Wine* (London: Chatto & Windus, 1957).

Epilogue

1. T. Schelling, personal communication. For a general discussion of death and decision making, see T. Schelling, "Strategic Relationships and Dying," in *Death and Decision*, ed. E. McMullin (Boulder, CO: Westview Press, 1978), 63–73.

2. C. M. Gillmore, "A Modern-Day Parable," *The American Psychologist* 26 (1971): 314.

*Index

*

About the Author

Ellen J. Langer is Professor of Psychology at Harvard University. She is Chair of the Social Psychology Program and a member of the Division on Aging of the Faculty of Medicine at Harvard. The recipient of a Guggenheim Fellowship, Professor Langer is the author of over seventy-five journal articles and chapters in scholarly works. Her other books include *The Power of Mindful Learning*, *Personal Politics* (with Carol Dweck), and *The Psychology of Control*. In 1988, she received the Award for Distinguished Contributions to Psychology in the Public Interest of the American Psychological Association.